Mesopotamian Myths

A Captivating Guide to Myths from Mesopotamia and Sumerian Mythology

© Copyright 2019

All Rights Reserved. No part of this book may be reproduced in any form without permission in writing from the author. Reviewers may quote brief passages in reviews.

Disclaimer: No part of this publication may be reproduced or transmitted in any form or by any means, mechanical or electronic, including photocopying or recording, or by any information storage and retrieval system, or transmitted by email without permission in writing from the publisher.

While all attempts have been made to verify the information provided in this publication, neither the author nor the publisher assumes any responsibility for errors, omissions or contrary interpretations of the subject matter herein.

This book is for entertainment purposes only. The views expressed are those of the author alone, and should not be taken as expert instruction or commands. The reader is responsible for his or her own actions.

Adherence to all applicable laws and regulations, including international, federal, state and local laws governing professional licensing, business practices, advertising and all other aspects of doing business in the US, Canada, UK or any other jurisdiction is the sole responsibility of the purchaser or reader.

Neither the author nor the publisher assumes any responsibility or liability whatsoever on behalf of the purchaser or reader of these materials. Any perceived slight of any individual or organization is purely unintentional.

Free Bonus from Captivating History (Available for a Limited time)

Hi History Lovers!

Now you have a chance to join our exclusive history list so you can get your first history ebook for free as well as discounts and a potential to get more history books for free! Simply visit the link below to join.

Captivatinghistory.com/ebook

Also, make sure to follow us on Facebook, Twitter and Youtube by searching for Captivating History.

Contents

PART 1: MESOPOTAMIAN MYTHOLOGY 0
INTRODUCTION 1
PART I: CREATION MYTHS 5
PART II: TALES OF GODS AND GODDESSES 30
PART III: SELECTIONS FROM THE *EPIC OF GILGAMESH* 51
GLOSSARY 79
PART 2: SUMERIAN MYTHOLOGY 85
INTRODUCTION 86
PART I: TALES OF GODS AND GODDESSES 90
ENKI AND NINMAH 90
ENLIL AND NINLIL 93
ENKI AND NINHURSAG 97
THE EXPLOITS OF NINURTA 104
THE JOURNEY OF NANNA TO NIPPUR 111
INANNA AND EBIH 115
DUMUZI AND ENKIMDU 119
THE MARRIAGE OF MARTU 121

PART II: TALES OF KINGS AND HEROES	125
ENMERKAR AND THE ENSUHKESHDANNA	125
LUGALBANDA IN THE MOUNTAIN CAVE	130
LUGALBANDA AND THE ANZU BIRD	135
THE SUMERIAN GILGAMESH	141
PART I: INANNA AND THE HULUPPU TREE	141
PART II: ENKIDU IN THE UNDERWORLD	144
PART III: GILGAMESH AND HUWAWA	150
PART IV: GILGAMESH AND AGA	158
SARGON AND UR-ZABABA	161
BIBLIOGRAPHY	167
GLOSSARY	171

Part 1: Mesopotamian Mythology
A Captivating Guide to Ancient Near Eastern Myths

Introduction

The civilizations that grew up in the Tigris and Euphrates River Valleys many thousands of years ago have left important legacies: agriculture, mathematics, astronomy, the wheel, and writing. The ancient Sumerian culture was one of the first to create a method of recording thoughts and data in a more or less permanent form, and other peoples who came into contact with the Sumerians adopted this idea for their own uses. Not only did they adopt technological advances, but also there was a great deal of interplay between Sumerian mythology and storytelling and that of Mesopotamian culture, generally.

Starting around 2300 BCE, Akkadian became the standard language of the Mesopotamian region, and it was split into three dialects: spoken Akkadian fell into either the northern or Assyrian dialect, or the southern or Babylonian dialect, while a third literary dialect was in use for written works and thus was accessible only to the educated. A Semitic language that is related to modern Arabic, Amharic, and Hebrew, Akkadian was used to record business transactions, laws, history and pseudo-history, mythology, and heroic epics. It was the language of trade and diplomacy for a wide geographical area as well, extending both into a large part of western

Asia and even into northwest Africa. For example, we have surviving pedagogical documents showing that scribes in ancient Egypt might be expected to learn to read and write Akkadian as part of their duties.

Mesopotamia also was the scene for a series of imperial projects, starting with the Akkadian Empire under Sargon of Akkad in the 24th century BCE. Akkad was a city-state, the exact location of which has yet to be determined, and from this base Sargon expanded his reach to other places including Sumer. After the fall of the Akkadian Empire, the city-states of Assur (the primary city of Assyria) in the north and Babylon in the south vied for control of the region, each having success at various times.

Because of the linguistic, political, and religious intermingling of speakers of the Akkadian language, it is very difficult to separate out specific religious or mythological traditions for any of these three cultures, with certain exceptions. We know that the principal deity of Assyria was the god Assur, and the principal deity of Babylon was Marduk. There are certain creation legends that can be connected specifically with Babylon because of the primacy of Marduk in those tales, and certain prayers and incantations addressed to Assur that obviously come from Assyria, but it is otherwise extremely difficult to parse which mythographic bits came from which culture due to the roster of shared divinities in the pantheon, the sharing of myths, and the commonalities of religious practices among Mesopotamian peoples. The waters are further muddied by the integration of Sumerian, Assyrian, and Babylonian mythographic practices; many of the clay tablets containing these stories are bilingual, in both Sumerian and Akkadian, while myths in these languages also contain many parallels in terms of character, theme, and plot.

Surviving documents in Akkadian principally are in cuneiform writing on clay tablets. The word "cuneiform" comes from the Latin *cuneus*, which means "wedge," referring to the use of a wedge-shaped stylus to impress symbols into wet clay. The Sumerians originated this form of writing, which was later adapted for the

Akkadian language. A significant number of literary texts come from royal libraries that were compiled by the Assyrian king Sennacherib (705–681 BCE) and Ashurbanipal (r. 668–c. 627 BCE), the king of the so-called Neo-Assyrian Empire. The ruins of these libraries, in what is now Iraq, were discovered by archaeologists in the mid-nineteenth century, and until that time, writings from these ancient civilizations had been lost to history. Therefore, the modern discipline of Assyriology (a blanket term for studies of the ancient Near East) is less than two hundred years old, and more is yet to be discovered from the fragments that have been excavated (or pillaged) from the remains of these ancient civilizations. One recent discovery from 2015 is a new segment of the *Epic of Gilgamesh*.

This present volume of Mesopotamian myths is divided into three sections. The first of these contains creation myths, the most extended of which is the *Enuma Elish*, or Babylonian creation story. In this myth, the god Marduk does battle with the dragon Tiamat, and from her body and that of her second-in-command, he creates the world. The story of Atrahasis involves not original creation but re-creation, since this is the myth of the Great Flood that the gods send to wash everything away. The good man Atrahasis is spared only by the intervention of the god Enki, who forewarns Atrahasis and tells him to build the ark that will save him, his family, and the animals. Etana's tale is less cosmic in nature than the preceding two stories: the act of creation involved is Etana's attempt to have a child and thus an heir to his throne.

The deeds and foibles of the Mesopotamian gods are on display in the second section, in stories that inform us about the characters of these divinities and which contain themes that tell us something about Mesopotamian concepts of cosmic order. In the first story, the goddess Ishtar decides to visit the Underworld where the goddess Ereshkigal holds sway. When Ereshkigal worries that Ishtar plans to supplant her, she sets a trap that holds Ishtar prisoner until she is rescued. Ereshkigal's deed has cosmic implications: since Ishtar is a fertility goddess, her imprisonment means that procreation on Earth is suspended.

Ereshkigal is a primary figure in the next story as well, which tells how Nergal, god of war and pestilence, comes to be her consort. Nergal manages to refuse all of the blandishments Ereshkigal puts before him, except for the enticement of her body. Having given into his desire, Nergal must make the Underworld his abode and remain there as Ereshkigal's lover or else Ereshkigal will overturn the natural order by sending the dead onto the Earth to eat the living.

Divine and natural order are also themes of the last two stories in this section. In the first, the hero-god Ninurta does his own work of restoring divine order when he defeats the Anzu Bird who steals the Tablets of Destiny from Ellil, while the myth about Adapa functions as a just-so story explaining why humans are not immortal.

Perhaps the most famous of all Mesopotamian myths is the *Epic of Gilgamesh*, an extended narrative about the exploits of Gilgamesh, king of Uruk, and his wild-man friend, Enkidu. If the stories of the gods told in the first two sections function as explanations about cosmic order, the themes of *Gilgamesh* center on the internal order of human beings, focusing on the deep love and friendship between Enkidu and Gilgamesh, on human fears about mortality, and the human desire for eternal life.

Mesopotamian myths are some of the oldest written stories in the world, and although in modern history we have only had the privilege of knowing them for less than two hundred years, they nevertheless speak to us about things that are basic to the human condition. Love, hate, creation, destruction, desire, sorrow, and fear are all universal human experiences and have been since the beginning of time, as is the human wish to project these things onto beings that are larger than life in order to explain how the world came to be the way it is.

Part I: Creation Myths

The Creation of the World

The Babylonian creation myth is preserved in cuneiform writing on seven clay tablets and has come to be known as the Enuma Elish, *after the first two words of the epic. In ancient times, this important myth was recited annually on the Babylonian New Year in honor of Marduk, the primary Babylonian god, who defeats the rebellious goddess Tiamat and her general, the god Qingu. Marduk then uses the bodies of his slain enemies to create the heavens and the Earth, and to make human beings to serve the gods.*

Unfortunately, the tablets that preserve the Enuma Elish *are broken and incomplete, so much of the original poem is missing. However, the poem tends to repeat large sections of text, so what is missing from one point in the story sometimes can be recreated or inferred from another. The myth recounts the emergence or creation of several named gods, the most important of whom are Marduk and his father, Ea. In addition to Marduk and his immediate ancestors, many other gods both named and unnamed have roles in this tale, but their origin stories are not told here.*

In the time when the heavens above had no name and the Earth beneath had no name, there was only Apsu, the one who begat the heavens and the Earth, and with Apsu was Tiamat, who gave birth to them. And in this time, the waters mingled together, the sweet water that was Apsu and the salt that was Tiamat, but neither was there pasture nor reeded marsh, nor had any of the gods yet been begotten or given names.

Then it happened that the gods came into being. First among them were Lahmu and Lahamu, brother and sister, the children of Apsu and Tiamat, and Lahmu and Lahamu together are the constellations in the sky. From Lahmu and Lahamu came Anshar and Kishar, brother and sister, god of the sky and goddess of the Earth. If Lahmu and Lahamu were great, Anshar and Kishar were greater yet, greater of stature, greater of strength.

From Anshar and Kishar came Anu, the very equal of his divine father, and Anu begat Ea, the god of the waters of the Tigris and the Euphrates. Ea was even greater than his own father, was even mightier than his own grandfather, and the wisdom of Ea knew no bounds.

Together Ea and his brother gods roared up and down the divine abode. Such a clamor they made that it disturbed Tiamat. In the face of their doings, Tiamat held her peace, although she detested their acts. Such a noise the brother gods made that even Apsu could not make himself heard above it, and so Apsu called to himself Mummu, his adviser, and said, "Good Mummu, let us go to Tiamat and take counsel together. We must decide what to do with these gods who roar up and down our divine abode."

And so Mummu and Apsu went to Tiamat, and Apsu said, "We must have order! We must have peace! Surely I should destroy these brother gods who roar up and down our divine abode."

But Tiamat replied, "Destruction is too harsh a solution. We should not destroy what we ourselves have created. Let us deal kindly with the brother gods, to make them stop their roaring about."

Mummu spoke next. "Yes, O Apsu, O radiant one, surely you must destroy these gods. Destroy them all! Then you will have peace, then you will have order in the divine abode."

Then Apsu rejoiced, for he knew that Mummu spoke the truth. Apsu rejoiced and plotted to kill all his children, and Mummu fell upon Apsu's neck and embraced him.

But the plans of Apsu did not go unnoticed. Ea learned of what Apsu meant to do and vowed to put a stop to the destruction of the brother gods. Ea crafted a great spell, a powerful spell, a holy spell of sleep, and he cast it upon Apsu. Apsu was powerless to resist the incantation, and soon he fell into a deep slumber. When Ea saw that Apsu was overcome with sleep, he went to Apsu and took from him his diadem and put it upon his own brow. Ea bound Apsu with strong bonds, and then Ea slew that elder god. Ea slew Apsu, the father of all the gods, and then he fell upon Mummu and bound him in chains and threw him into a strong room, locking the door so that there should be no escape.

Then it was that Ea founded a divine abode of his own. He founded this abode and called it the *Apsu*. Within this abode, Ea made a chamber, a chamber for himself and for his wife, Damkina. And there it was in the abode called the Apsu that Marduk was begotten. Ea was his father, and Damkina was his mother. Marduk, the greatest of gods, was begotten there, and his father Ea delighted in him. Ea bestowed great majesty and strength upon Marduk, making him not only the equal of the other gods but their superior. Well made in his body was Marduk, with comely limbs. Four eyes had Marduk, and four ears, and from his mouth shot flames of fire. Large were his eyes and ears, and his body was exceeding tall, and he was named Son of the Sun and Sun of the Heavens, and his father Ea delighted in him greatly.

Anu, god of the sky and father of Ea, fashioned the four winds. Anu took these winds and gave them to his grandson, Marduk. Anu gave the winds to Marduk, and with these Marduk called up a mighty storm. The storm made waves upon waves, and this disturbed Tiamat greatly.

The other gods saw what was done, and they went to Tiamat, saying, "Did not Ea destroy Apsu, your divine spouse? Did he not imprison Mummu, Apsu's wise counsellor? And so it is that now we cannot sleep. And so it is that we have no rest. Come! Let us go into battle! Let us avenge Apsu and Mummu and recover our peace that we may rest."

And so the gods went aside to plan their battle.

But Tiamat, for her part, engendered great monsters, strong beasts and fell, that they might avenge her divine spouse, that they might destroy Ea and thus punish him for his deeds. Tiamat brought forth dragons, beasts with poisonous sharp teeth, creatures so fearsome that even the bravest would die if they but saw them. Dragons Tiamat brought forth, and many other beasts besides: lions and scorpion-men, wild dogs and demons, and a great bull. Eleven of these beasts Tiamat brought forth, but she gave the headship to none of these, preferring instead to bestow it on her son, Qingu. To him, Tiamat gave the three Tablets of Destiny, that he might have the power to overthrow Ea.

Then Tiamat said to Qingu, "Go! Lead the army of fell beasts! Lead the army of gods who are our allies! Bring battle to Ea, and avenge my divine spouse!"

Word of what Tiamat had done came to Ea, and he despaired. Surely he would never defeat such an army, headed by such a captain. Ea went to his grandfather, Anshar, and said, "Woe! Tiamat has created an army of eleven fell beasts, and of many gods, with Qingu at their head, and he bears the Tablets of Destiny. Surely we will never prevail against such a foe!"

Anshar said, "No, we shall not falter! You yourself slew Apsu, Tiamat's divine spouse. Any foe that faces you surely will be defeated. Go into battle!"

And so Ea set out to do battle with Tiamat. He found the place where she was with her army, and when he saw how very great the fell monsters were, with Qingu at their head, he grew greatly afraid, and he turned back.

"O my father," said Ea, "I set out on my road to do battle with Tiamat, but woe! Her power is too much for me. I shall never be able to defeat her. Send someone else instead."

Then Anshar turned to Anu and said, "O my son, my firstborn! You who are hero and warrior, no one may withstand your strength. Go you and fight Tiamat and her army! Surely you shall return victorious!"

And so Anu set out to do battle with Tiamat, but when he saw what she had prepared against him, his heart quailed, and he turned back.

"O my father," said Anu, "I set out on my road to do battle with Tiamat, but woe! Her power is too much for me. I shall never be able to defeat her. Perhaps you yourself should go."

Anshar called to himself all the gods. He told them of Tiamat's plans and of the army she had created, how they purposed to destroy all the other gods in revenge for the death of Apsu. But none of the other gods would take up the quest to defeat her. They all sat silent and afraid.

It was then that Ea summoned his son, Marduk. Together they went into Ea's chamber to take counsel together. Ea said, "Only you may stand against Tiamat and her fell beasts. Go before Anshar. Declare yourself our champion. Only you can save us!"

Obedient to his father, Marduk went before Anshar and the other gods. There he declared himself their champion, there he offered to meet Tiamat and her fell beasts, with Qingu at their head. Then the gods rejoiced and declared a feast, a feast to celebrate Marduk, their champion, before he went into battle. And when the feast was done, they said, "Marduk our champion shall be first among us! To you shall be the sovereignty over all that is, and even the gods shall bow down to you."

And so it was that Marduk readied himself for war. He took up his great bow and a quiver of arrows. He took up his mighty spear and his massive club. He took up lightning and filled his whole body with flame. He commanded the winds to help him, the four winds and the seven winds. These and other winds besides he called to him, to come with him and to wreak havoc on Tiamat. To his chariot he harnessed four steeds, swift as arrows and fierce as lions. Thus prepared, Marduk set out for battle in his chariot pulled by war stallions, with the winds at his command.

Qingu heard the approach of Marduk and saw him thus arrayed for battle, and his heart quailed. Seeing their leader's distress, the eleven fell beasts also despaired, but Tiamat gathered her courage and spoke words of rebellion to Marduk.

Marduk was not swayed by the words of Tiamat. He said to her, "You have rebelled against Anu, against the gods themselves. You have prepared an army to destroy them. But I say to you that we should settle this between ourselves. Let us meet in single combat, you and I, and that way decide who may have the victory."

For answer, Tiamat screamed her battle cry and ran at Marduk, thinking to destroy him where he stood. Not fearing her at all, Marduk held his ground. He took up a great net and threw it over Tiamat, entangling her so that she could not move. Then Marduk sent an evil wind to blow in Tiamat's face, to force open her mouth and to distend her body so that she could not speak. When that was done, Marduk nocked an arrow to his bow and shot Tiamat. The arrow entered her and clove her heart in two.

When Tiamat's army saw what had befallen the goddess, the eleven beasts fled the field. The gods who had followed Tiamat trembled and tried to flee, but Marduk caught them all in his net and threw them into prison. The demons also that had followed in Tiamat's train Marduk captured, and he hunted down the eleven beasts and cast them into fetters. Last of all, Marduk captured Qingu. Marduk took from him the Tablets of Destiny and fastened them upon his own breast.

Then Marduk went to the body of the slain Tiamat. With his great club, Marduk crushed her skull. He cut open the vessels of her body and let the North Wind take her blood away. The other gods rejoiced at Marduk's victory, giving him many fine gifts and praising him well.

But Marduk's work was not yet done. He took Tiamat's body and cut it in half along its length. One half of her body he set above to be the sky. Marduk posted two guardians to watch that portion of Tiamat, to make sure that the waters it contained did not escape. This done, Marduk went into the heavens, and there he created an abode for the gods. This abode he built neighboring the Apsu that his father Ea had made, and Marduk called his dwelling the *E-sara*. The E-sara was made to be even greater than the Apsu, and within the E-sara, Marduk made dwelling places for his grandfather, Anu, and for his father, Ea, and for Ellil, the god of the winds.

That done, Marduk began a new work. In the sky, he placed the stars in their courses; he made the twelve creatures of the Zodiac and put them in their rightful places. Marduk divided the times and the seasons, he created the calendar of months and days, and to watch over this, he placed Nibiru [the planet Jupiter]. Marduk created Nanna, the moon-god, and commanded him to shine at his proper time. To Nanna, Marduk gave the keeping of time, the measure of the months, and the times and places he should stand in relation to Shamash, the sun-god, and thus it was that Marduk established the turnings of the night and the day and the turnings of the months and the years.

From Tiamat's body, Marduk made the waters. He made the rain and the mist; he filled the abyss with the waters from her head. Two rivers he made flow from her eyes, the great rivers of the Tigris and the Euphrates, and from her breasts, Marduk wrought the mountains.

And so it was that from Tiamat's body was made the substance of the Earth.

When all was ready, Marduk gave the guiding of the world to his father Ea, and to his grandfather, Anu, he gave the Tablets of Destiny that he had taken from Qingu. The eleven fell beasts made by Tiamat he bound, and he made statues of them to guard the gates of the Apsu.

Seeing all that Marduk had done, all the gods rejoiced. They proclaimed the glory of his name; they gave him rich gifts. The gods all bowed down to Marduk and honored him greatly. They clothed him in clean robes and anointed him with fragrant oil. They gave to him the keeping of their holy places, and they said to him, "You alone shall be our king! Whatever you command, thus shall we do!"

Then Marduk said, "The Apsu I have made secure, and the E-sara I have made to be your abode. But another palace shall I yet create, the place where the gods shall gather to take counsel together. This place shall I call *Babylon*. In Babylon shall we make feast, and in Babylon shall we receive the offerings that we are due."

And the council of the gods said, "Yes, all these things you should do, for you are our king, and we shall have none other. Let it be done as you say."

When things had been set in order in the heavens and on the Earth, Marduk bent his thought to the creation of other things, of things that might live and move upon the Earth. "I shall make a creature," said Marduk, "I shall make it of bone and of blood, and its duty shall be to provide for the gods. This creature I shall call 'man,' and I shall make it to live upon the Earth."

Then Marduk turned to the council of the gods and said, "Tell me, who was it that told Tiamat to rise in rebellion against us? Whose words swayed her and caused her to bring battle?"

The gods answered Marduk, saying, "Qingu it was who fomented rebellion, and Qingu it was who told Tiamat to bring battle."

Thus it was that Qingu was brought before Marduk and the council of the gods. Bound in fetters, Qingu was brought before them, and sentence was passed upon him. Marduk opened the vessels of his body, and from his blood, Marduk fashioned human beings to be the servants of the gods.

The heavens and the Earth had been created, and the sun and the moon given their duties. Human beings had been created to serve the gods, and all had been set in order except for the council of the gods themselves. Marduk divided the gods into companies and told them where they were to dwell. Three hundred he made to guard the heavens, and six hundred he sent to the Earth and to the Underworld.

When that was done, the gods turned to Marduk and said, "O King, you have done a great work. You have made all that is. You have created human beings to do service for us. What now might we do for you in return?"

Marduk was greatly pleased by what the gods had said, and he replied, "Create Babylon! Make for us a shrine in which we might repose ourselves."

The gods accepted this task with a good will. They went to work making bricks, and from the bricks, they made a city, and within the city, a great shrine was built, a high tower that was to be a temple where Marduk might reside along with Ea, Ellil, and Anu. For themselves also they built temples, that they might have places of repose.

Babylon soon was finished, a great and shining city with a fine temple to the gods. Marduk was well pleased with this work, and he said, "Well done, well done, my brother gods! Let us now have a feast! Let us eat and drink to celebrate our creations and to celebrate our new shrine in which we might repose."

The whole company of the gods sat down with Marduk to a feast. They ate and drank to their hearts' content. They rejoiced in the making of their new city and their new shrines. When the feasting was over, the gods took a solemn oath to Marduk, proclaiming him their king and judge, giving over to him dominion of all things. They also made commandments for the proper care for the gods and of the work that human beings ought to do in honor of all the deities. The gods all praised Marduk for his glory, calling upon him by his many names: Wise in Counsel, Great Provider, Lord of Life, Creator of All Things, and many other great names besides, all the fifty names of the great god Marduk, the mighty one and hero, who made the heavens and the Earth, who set the gods in their abodes, and who made human beings to be their servants.

Atrahasis

Many cultures have narratives of a great flood that wipes away all life with the exception of a few righteous survivors, and ancient Mesopotamian culture was no different. There are several different versions of the Flood narrative in both Sumerian and Akkadian; one such survives within the context of the Gilgamesh epic. The retelling presented below is based on the Old Babylonian version, which dates from the 17th century BCE, according to Benjamin Foster in his translation of the tale.

In the beginning of the world, there were no people. Only the gods walked the Earth, and the gods themselves had to work for their sustenance. The Annunaki themselves, the greater gods, had to dig the canals, till the fields, tend the beasts, and bring in the harvests.

"This work is too much," said the Annunaki. "Our backs bend under this heavy load. We must get someone else to do this for us."

And so the Annunaki decided that they would go up into the sky. First they cast lots to see where they would go. Anu the Father of All went up into the sky. Ellil took the Earth for his domain, and Enki took the sea. Then the Annunaki made the Igigi, the lesser gods, do all of the work that they had formerly done. They made the Igigi dig the canals, till the fields, tend the beasts, and bring in the harvests.

The first deed of the Igigi was to dig the riverbed for the Tigris. Then they dug the bed for the Euphrates. They set up the Apsu, the home of the gods, on their lands. For forty years, the Igigi labored at the Annunaki's command, and finally they had had enough of it. "Let us go to Ellil and throw him down. We will throw him down from his seat, and he will no longer have dominion over us. We will bring battle to his gates and overthrow him, and then we will be free!"

The Igigi made a great pyre of their work tools and set it ablaze. Then they took up their weapons, and in the middle of the night they marched on the E-kur, the house of Ellil. Ellil did not know of the approach of the Igigi, but Kalkal, a servant of Ellil, had done his duty well and had barred the gates of the E-kur long since. Kalkal saw the approach of the Igigi. He went to Nusku, another servant of Ellil, and told him, "Go to our master. Rouse him. Let him know that a great mob is approaching the E-kur. They will surround us. Tell Ellil, quickly!"

Nusku ran to Ellil's chamber and told him about the mob that was surrounding the E-kur. "Take up weapons!" said Ellil. "Take up your weapons, and stand in front of me. Bar the door to my chamber, but you stand between it and me, with your weapons at the ready!"

Nusku looked at Ellil and said, "O my master, why are you so pale? What is it you fear from those who are outside our walls? If you are so afraid, summon Anu to your aid! Summon Enki to your aid! Surely they will help you."

Ellil summoned Anu, and he summoned Enki. Anu said, "What is it? Why do you summon us?"

Ellil said, "Look about you! Look how the rabble surround my home! Look how they pound at my gates! What am I to do about this? These are my own children, risen up against me! My own children have taken up weapons, and they have laid siege to my home."

"Do you know what it is they want?" said Anu. "Why are they here? Maybe you should find that out first. Send Nusku out to them. Have Nusku ask them what they want of you and why they have taken up weapons against you. Send him in the name of the Annunaki."

Nusku went to the gate. He opened it and stood before the Igigi. He bowed to them and said, "I am here in the name of Anu, your father; and of Ellil, warrior and counsellor; and of Ninurta, your chamberlain; and of Ennugi, who controls the canals. I am here in their name to ask you why you are here and what you want. Who started this? Who decided that you should take up weapons and surround the house of Ellil? Speak! Tell me why you are here."

The Igigi answered, one and all, "Together we decided to take up weapons. Together we decided to lay siege to the house of Ellil. The Annunaki set us to work for them. Hard and long has been our labor. Our backs are bent, and our bodies are weary. We have had enough! And so we bring battle to the gates of the E-kur. We will fight for our freedom!"

Nusku went back to Ellil and told him what the Igigi had said. Ellil wept when he heard the plight of the Igigi. "O father Anu," he said, "can nothing be done to help my children? Can nothing be done to ease their burdens?"

Anu summoned together the council of the Annunaki, that they might discover what ought to be done about the plight of the Igigi. Enki spoke before the council, saying, "Yes, we ought to help the Igigi. Truly we gave them a burden that is too heavy for them. I know what we ought to do. We should create human beings. We should create them and give the labor of the Igigi to them." Enki turned to Mami, the mother-goddess, and said, "O Mami, could you create human beings? Could you make them, so that we might give to them the labor of the Igigi?"

But Mami replied, "This is not for me to do. You must be the one to create the humans. But if you give me clay, I will shape them."

"Very well," said Enki. "This is what I shall do: I will make a bath of purification on the first, seventh, and fifteenth days of the month, so that the gods might be purified. One god shall we sacrifice, and his blood will be mixed with Mami's clay."

And so this was done. The Annunaki made the purification baths, and they sacrificed Aw-ila, who gave himself for this purpose. Mami took the clay and mixed it with Aw-ila's blood, and so it was that the human being had also a spirit, because it was made with the blood of a god.

When the clay was well mixed with the blood, Enki called together the whole assembly of the gods. The Annunaki came at Enki's summons, and they spat upon the clay. The Igigi came at Enki's summons, and they spat upon the clay. Then Mami said to the whole assembly, "I have completed the task that you set me. Here is the clay that has the blood and the spirit of a god. From this, I will make beings to take upon them your labor and your pain. Before you is the beginning of new creatures, creatures who also may bewail their lot, who also may weary our ears with their clamoring."

Hearing this, the Igigi surged forward and fell at Mami's feet. They kissed her feet, saying, "We called you Mami, but now you shall be known as Mistress of All the Gods."

Enki and Mami summoned fourteen goddesses who would bear the new beings. While Enki trod the clay, kneading it with his feet, Mami said an incantation. When the clay was well mixed and the incantation done, Mami divided the clay into fourteen portions. Seven pieces she set on the right, and seven she set on the left. Seven pieces of clay were given to seven of the goddesses, and the beings they bore became males. The other seven pieces of clay were given to the other seven goddesses, and the beings they bore became females.

Mami told the new beings that they should each choose another to be their mate, one male with one female. She instructed them on how to live, and how they would bear their children, and on the proper reverence to the gods.

And so it was that the new men and women were put upon the Earth, and to them was given the labor that the gods had done. The new men and women dug the canals, tilled the fields, tended the beasts, and brought in the harvests. The new men and women did this labor, and they also married and had many fine children.

Twelve hundred years went by. The new human beings did their labor, and they had their children, and their children had children, and on and on this went until the Earth was well covered with human beings, and the noise of their clamoring rose up into the heavens, offending the ears of the gods.

"Oh!" cried Ellil. "This cannot stand. The noise of these beings is too much. I cannot sleep because of their din. We should diminish them. Let us make a plague, and send it upon them. Let us send a plague to kill them and diminish their numbers, and diminish their noise thereby."

The other gods readily agreed to this. "Yes, let us send a plague. Truly there are too many people, and truly they make such a din that none of us can sleep. Let us send a plague!"

And so the gods sent a plague upon the people. The plague swept through the land, and many died. Men, women, and children, young and old, all fell victim. One among them who survived was a wise man named Atrahasis. He was a devout man, speaking often with the god Enki. In turn, Enki honored Atrahasis by speaking with him.

"O Enki!" cried Atrahasis. "How long must we suffer like this? How long will the gods afflict us with this plague? Our children are dying, and our elders. Wives are leaving their husbands widowers, and husbands widow their wives. Help us! What can we do to appease the gods?"

"Call together the council of elders," said Enki. "Call them together, and tell them that they must all forgo the worship of their own gods.

Instead, they must build a temple for Namtar, god of plagues. For him must they bake bread, and to his temple must they bring it. When he sees the fine gift of bread laid at his door, perhaps he will feel ashamed and stop the plague."

Atrahasis did as Enki instructed. He told the elders what must be done. Together the people built a great temple to Namtar. They baked bread for him and laid it at the door of the temple. Namtar smelled the perfume of the baking bread. He saw how well crafted the loaves were and how many had been laid at the door of his temple. He felt ashamed for having afflicted the people, and so he withdrew the plague from them. Those who had been stricken began to get well again, and no one else fell ill.

Twelve hundred years went by after the end of the plague. The people did their labor, and they had their children, and their children had children, and on and on this went until the Earth was well covered with human beings, and the noise of their clamoring rose up into the heavens, offending the ears of the gods.

"Oh!" cried Ellil. "This cannot stand. The noise of these beings is too much. I cannot sleep because of their din. We should diminish them. Let us make a drought, and send it upon them. Let us send a drought so that their crops will not flourish. They will starve, and diminish their numbers, and diminish their noise thereby."

The other gods readily agreed to this. "Yes, let us send a drought. Truly there are too many people, and truly they make such a din that none of us can sleep. Let us send a drought!"

The gods called upon Adad, god of rain. "Stop the rain, Adad," said the gods. "Stop the rain so that the Earth dries up, so that the crops will not grow. That way the people will starve, and they will die, and finally it will be quiet enough for us to sleep."

And so Adad held back the rain. Drought came upon the land. The crops dried up, and the people thirsted, and soon many and many died.

The wise man Atrahasis again went to Enki and said, "How long must we suffer like this? How long will the gods afflict us with this drought? Our children are dying, and our elders. Wives are leaving their husbands widowers, and husbands widow their wives. Help us! What can we do to appease the gods?"

"Call together the council of elders," said Enki. "Call them together, and tell them that they must all forgo the worship of their own gods. Instead, they must build a temple for Adad, the rain-god. For him must they bake bread, and to his temple must they bring it. When he sees the fine gift of bread laid at his door, perhaps he will feel ashamed and stop the drought."

Atrahasis did as Enki instructed. He told the elders what must be done. Together the people built a great temple to Adad. They baked bread for him and laid it at the door of the temple. Adad smelled the perfume of the baking bread. He saw how well crafted the loaves were and how many had been laid at the door of his temple. He felt ashamed for having afflicted the people, and so he withdrew the drought from them. He gave them rain in plenty and morning dew. Soon the fields were bearing crops, and there was a plentiful harvest. Hunger and thirst were gone from the land.

Again the people became too noisy for the gods, and again the gods sent plague upon them. Again the gods sent plague, and when the numbers of the people were reduced, the gods relented.

After the plague was banished from the land, the people increased, and once again they disturbed the gods with their noise and bustle. Again the gods sent drought, and when the numbers of the people were reduced, the gods relented.

Twice the gods sent plague and then removed it. Twice the gods sent drought and then removed it. But after every plague and drought abated, the people increased their numbers until the din of their living echoed through the House of the Gods and the gods could no longer sleep.

Finally Ellil called together the Annunaki. He called them to a council and said, "Something must be done about the racket the people make. They are so noisy, none of us can sleep! We have tried plague. We have tried drought. Neither of those worked for long. We must do something more, something that will wipe out the people, so that we can sleep. I wish to bring a great flood upon the land. That will wipe out all the people, and at last we shall have peace."

Enki stood in council and cried out against this plan. "This is an evil thing you do, Ellil! Why should we wipe out all the people? Why should I desire to slay all of my children? Do this deed if you must, but I will have no part of it!"

And so Enki resolved to save at least some of the people from the wrath of Ellil and the Annunaki. Enki went to the wise man Atrahasis and sent to him a dream. Enki came to Atrahasis at night while he was sleeping, and he said, "Atrahasis! A great flood is coming, one that will wipe out every living thing. But I, Enki, your god, command you. Make a boat. Build it well, and seal it with pitch. Build it with many decks. Build it long, and build it wide. Take with you on your boat as many living things as you can. Seven days have you, before the flood arrives. Go and do my bidding, if you would live!"

Atrahasis woke from his dream. He straightway began building his boat, and his family helped him. Soon the great boat was built and provisioned, and Atrahasis filled it with the animals as Enki had commanded him to do. When the boat was ready, Atrahasis brought his family aboard. They sat down to a meal together, but Atrahasis was restless. He could not sit still. He could not eat or drink. He kept going outside and looking to see whether the flood was coming. Although he had built the boat that would save him, his heart was wretched, and he was sore afraid.

Atrahasis watched the skies. As he watched them, they grew dark with clouds, darker than Atrahasis had ever seen. Adad rode in those clouds, and he unleashed their rains upon the earth. Atrahasis went back into his boat and sealed up the doors with pitch.

The Anzu Bird roared through the sky. He rent the sky with his talons. And then it was that the flood came forth. It rushed out over the land in a great wall, washing away everything in its path. So great was the deluge that even the gods became frightened and hid within the walls of their House. Enki wailed in mourning for the death of all his children.

The entire world was scoured clean by the flood, and soon the Annunaki and the Igigi became hungry. They became hungry because the flood had washed away everything. All the people were dead, and all the fields lay under a great depth of water. The great mother-goddess Mami lamented the destruction. "O that the day may never again break! Woe to me that I agreed to Ellil's chosen path! Would that Anu had intervened and checked Ellil's course as he ought to have done!"

Ellil looked out over what he had wrought, thinking that finally he would have peace. But then he spied the boat of Atrahasis, and he fell into a rage. "Look at that! Look, out on the water! There is a boat, and it is filled with people and animals! We gods agreed together that all living things were to be destroyed. We gods agreed together that nothing should survive this flood. Only Enki could have done this thing. Only Enki would dare go against the will of all the gods!"

"Yes, I did this thing," said Enki. "And I would do it again, a thousand times over. My work it is to see that life is protected. The flood was an evil deed, Ellil, for you have punished the just along with the unjust."

[The remainder of the tale is fragmentary, but apparently Enki and Nintu, the goddess of giving birth, work together to create new people and establish a new social order. One remaining fragment deals with assigning roles to women as the bearers of children and priestesses who are to remain childless.]

Etana

This story is set in Kish, which was an ancient Sumerian city-state in what is now Iraq, and is about Etana, who the story says was the first king of Kish. However, the Sumerian King List puts Etana as the thirteenth king of Kish, so it is possible that one purpose of this story was to bolster Etana's historical clout and claim to authority.

One important theme of this story is the relationship between parents and children. Etana has no children of his own, and this is a sorrow to him; part of the story deals with his attempts to get an heir. The two other main characters in the story are an eagle and a serpent, both of which have broods that they are raising. The eagle's youngest chick attempts to advise his parent, while the serpent's children all fall prey to the greedy eagle. The serpent duly punishes the eagle for his treachery, but the eagle's redemption is found when he assists Etana to get the plant that will allow him to have children of his own.

In the beginning, the gods created the Earth and filled it with people. The gods also created a great city, the city of Kish. The Annunaki laid the plans for the city, and the Igigi built it from good brick. When the city was built, the gods decreed a great feast for all the people, but the gods would not let them into the city for the people had no king to rule them and to establish order. The gods searched all the lands for a man to be king over the city and finally declared that Etana should be made king in Kish.

In thanksgiving for his kingship, Etana built a shrine to the rain-god Adad, whom Etana especially revered. Next to the shrine, Etana planted a poplar tree, and when it came into its growth, an eagle made its eyrie in the branches, and a serpent made its burrow in the roots. The eagle said to the serpent, "We are neighbors here, so let us also be friends."

The serpent replied, "This I cannot do, for you have transgressed against Shamash, the god of the sun. But if you will swear with me not to overstep the limits of Shamash, then we can be companions.

Let us swear that whoever oversteps the limits of Shamash receive a great punishment."

The eagle agreed to this, and so they both swore on the Underworld not to anger Shamash. The serpent and the eagle then worked together, taking it in turns to find prey and bring it back to their homes. When it was the eagle's day to hunt, he would find wild oxen and wild asses and bring them back to the tree, and the serpent and his children would eat of what the eagle brought. When it was the serpent's day to hunt, he would bring back deer and gazelles, and the eagle and his children would eat of what the serpent brought.

For a time, the eagle and the serpent lived in peace together, hunting their prey and feeding one another's children. But soon the eagle began to think ill of the serpent. He plotted in his heart to eat the serpent's children. The eagle said to his brood, "I have a mind to eat the serpent's children. Then the serpent will run away, and we shall have the whole tree to ourselves."

The smallest chick said to his father, "No, Father! This is an evil thought. You must not eat the serpent's children, for you swore an oath to Shamash to live in peace with the serpent. If you eat the serpent's children, surely Shamash will punish you most sorely!"

But the eagle did not listen to the words of the youngest chick. He waited until the serpent had gone out to hunt, and then he flew down to the roots of the tree and ate up all the young serpents. That evening, when the serpent returned with its kill, he looked in his burrow and found it empty. He looked at the ground outside the burrow and saw it scored with the marks of the eagle's talons.

The serpent mourned deeply. He wept bitter tears, mourning for his dead children. Then the serpent turned his eyes to the heavens and said, "O Shamash, look what has become of my family! I trusted the eagle, and we swore an oath together. I trusted him, and together we worked to feed our young. But the eagle has betrayed me. He has devoured all my children. They are dead and gone, but his fledglings grow and flourish. O Shamash, I ask you to take vengeance on the eagle for this deed and for breaking his solemn oath to you!"

Shamash saw the tears of the serpent and heard his words. He said, "This is what you shall do. Go out hunting. Find a fine wild ox, and kill it. When it is dead, cut open its belly, and hide yourself in its entrails. Soon the birds will see the dead ox and will come down to feast upon it, and the eagle will come down with them. When the eagle begins to eat of the entrails, seize him, cut off his wings, and pluck out his tail feathers. Then cast him into a pit, and leave him there to die of hunger and thirst."

The serpent did as Shamash commanded. He slew the ox and hid himself in the beast's entrails. The eagle saw the dead ox and said to his children, "Come, let us feast! There is a fine dead ox there, and we shall eat well!"

But the smallest chick said, "No, Father! You must not eat of that ox. What if the serpent is hiding inside it? Surely he is wroth that you devoured his young. He may have set a trap for you!"

The eagle did not listen to his chick. He flew down to the dead ox and began walking around it and on top of it, trying to find which was the best part to eat first. The eagle decided to go for the entrails, but when he was close enough, the serpent darted out from his covert and seized the eagle's wings.

"You invaded my burrow! You devoured my young!" shouted the serpent.

In great fear, the eagle cried, "Have mercy! Do not hurt me! If you let me go unharmed, I will reward you greatly!"

"I cannot let you go," said the serpent, "for in capturing you, I am following the command of Shamash himself, and if I do not do what he commands, I shall be punished. But I have done no wrong and deserve no punishment, while you have devoured my children and must pay for that deed!"

And so, the serpent cut off the eagle's wings and plucked out his tail feathers, then cast him into a pit and left him there to die. Every day, the eagle called to Shamash, saying, "Do not leave me here! Do not let me die in a pit! If you save me, I shall see to it that your name receives praise from every tongue of every creature!"

Shamash replied, "Why should I save you? You did a most evil thing. You devoured the serpent's children, and you broke the solemn oath you swore to me. I will not help you, but perhaps a mortal man will."

Now, at this time, Etana ruled over the city of Kish, and he had but one sorrow: he had no children of his own. Every day, Etana prayed to Shamash, saying, "O Shamash, listen to my prayer! I have fed you on the finest beasts of my flocks. I have poured the blood of my sacrifices out so that the Underworld might drink of it. I honor all the gods, and try to do right, but still I have no children. Mighty Shamash, I beg of you, reveal to me how I might have children. Reveal to me how I might get an heir. Show me where grows the plant of birth!"

Shamash heard the prayers of Etana and said to him, "Follow the road that leads into the mountains. You will find there a pit, and in the pit is an eagle. The eagle will show you where the plant is."

Etana did as Shamash commanded. He followed the road that led into the mountains, and there he found the pit. The eagle heard Etana's approach, and he cried out to Shamash, saying, "O mighty Shamash! Is this the man you promised would help me? Give to him the gift of understanding birds' speech, and let me understand his!"

Shamash did as the eagle asked. He gave the eagle the power to understand Etana's speech and gave Etana the power to understand what the eagle said. The eagle cried out from the bottom of the pit, "Tell me why you are here!"

"I am looking for the plant of birth," said Etana. "Mighty Shamash told me to come here. He said you would be able to help me. I am a king, but I have no heir, and it is a great sorrow to me."

"Help me," said the eagle, "and I will show you where the plant grows."

And so Etana helped the eagle. Every day, he brought food for the bird to eat, until its wings healed and its tail feathers grew back. Etana fed the eagle and taught it to fly again. For seven months, Etana fed the eagle and taught it to fly, and when the seven months were over, Etana helped the eagle out of the pit.

After Etana cared for him, the eagle was well and strong again. "I thank you for your help," said the eagle. "Tell me, how I may serve you, in return for your kindness?"

"Find for me the plant of birth that I might have an heir," said Etana.

The eagle flew up into the sky. He flew all around, but the plant was nowhere to be found. The eagle returned to Etana and said, "Maybe it would be better if you helped me search. Here, climb up on my back. We shall fly together, and search together. We shall go to Ishtar, the goddess of birth. Perhaps she will tell us where the plant is."

Etana mounted the back of the eagle. The eagle took flight, and when they were high in the sky, he cried out to Etana, "Look how small the Earth seems from up here! Look how small the sea appears!"

Higher and higher they flew, and the land and sea looked smaller and smaller, until finally they were so high that Etana could no longer see either the land or the sea, and he became very frightened indeed.

"My friend, set me down!" said Etana. "I do not wish to fly all the way up to heaven. Set me down, and let me return home to my city!"

The eagle dropped Etana off his back. Etana fell down one league, but then the eagle caught him with his wings. Then the eagle dropped Etana again and caught him again a league farther down. Once more the eagle dropped Etana and caught him when Etana was barely three cubits above the ground.

[Here there is a gap in the narrative. The story resumes with Etana telling the eagle about a dream he had.]

Etana said to the eagle, "My friend, I had a great dream last night. Surely it was sent by the gods. Let me tell you what happened. Together we went up to heaven, you and I. We came to the House of the Gods. First we went through the gates of Anu, Ellil, and Ea. Then we went through the gates of Sin, Shamash, Adad, and Ishtar. We bowed low before the gods, both you and I. After we passed through all the gates, we saw a house before us. We went into the house, and there was seated the most beautiful woman. She wore upon her head a shining crown. Also in the house was a finely carved throne, and under the throne there were three lions. I stepped toward the throne, but the lions sprang at me, and I woke up, shivering with fear."

"Oh!" said the eagle. "I know what this means. I must take you up to heaven. Climb on my back, and we will fly there together."

Etana mounted the back of the eagle. The eagle took flight, and when they were high in the sky, he cried out to Etana, "Look how small the Earth seems from up here! Look how small the sea appears!"

Higher and higher they flew, and the land and sea looked smaller and smaller, until finally they were so high that Etana could no longer see either the land or the sea. Higher and yet higher they flew until they arrived in heaven at the House of the Gods. Together Etana and the eagle went through the gates of Anu, Ellil, and Ea. Then they went through the gates of Sin, Shamash, Adad, and Ishtar. They bowed low before the gods together. After they passed through all the gates, they saw before them a house. They opened the door and went inside.

[The remainder of the story is missing, with the exception of a fragment that indicates Etana was able to obtain the plant of birth and return home with it.]

Part II: Tales of Gods and Goddesses

Ishtar Descends to the Underworld

This story explains what happens when the goddess Ishtar decides to pay a visit to the Underworld, which is ruled by Ereshkigal, her older sister and a rival goddess. It is somewhat unclear what Ishtar intends to accomplish by her visit, but Ereshkigal seems to be under the impression that Ishtar intends to supplant her. Ereshkigal therefore acts accordingly to strip Ishtar of her power by taking Ishtar's clothing and jewelry, piece by piece, so that the goddess must enter the Underworld as the human dead do, naked and alone.

Ishtar is a fertility goddess; when she is imprisoned by Ereshkigal, no procreation can take place upon the earth. The god Ea creates a beautiful eunuch named Asushunamir (although some translators state that this character may have been a male prostitute or transvestite) to trick Ereshkigal into letting Ishtar return to the world of the living. Assyriologist Benjamin R. Foster, in his translation of the story, notes that sending such a person would have been seen by Mesopotamian peoples as apropos, since Ishtar was the patron goddess of male prostitutes and transvestites, who worked as entertainers, and it is in this capacity that the eunuch enters the Underworld to trick Ereshkigal.

Two portions of the story seem to be omitted in the Akkadian version, and have been supplied from Foster's notes on the tale. These have to do with Asushunamir's interaction with Ereshkigal and with the reason why Tammuz is sent to the Underworld when Ishtar returns to the world of the living.

There came a time when the goddess Ishtar, daughter of the moon-god Sin, determined to go to the Underworld. She went to the Underworld, the place all enter but none leave, the place at which all roads end, a lightless place, and those who dwell therein eat clay and drink dust.

Ishtar went to the gates of the Underworld and said, "Gatekeeper, open the gate! Open for me, lest I break down these doors. Open for me, lest I raise the dead so that they might feed upon the living, and soon more shall be dead than alive. Open the gate!"

The gatekeeper said, "O Lady Ishtar, have patience, and wait a while. I must ask permission of my Lady Ereshkigal before opening to anyone, even to the Lady Ishtar."

The gatekeeper went to Ereshkigal and said, "O Lady Ereshkigal, your sister Ishtar waits at the gate of the Underworld and demands I open to her. The one who stirs up the deep in the sight of Ea is here and craves admittance."

Ereshkigal paled when she heard the gatekeeper's speech. "What might Ishtar hold against me that she visits me here? Shall I join the ones whose road has ended here? Shall I dwell in the place all enter but none leave? Shall I eat clay and drink dust? Shall I mourn for the young men torn from their brides and for the young women torn from their grooms? Shall I mourn for the stillborn and the infants who had so little of life?"

Then Ereshkigal said to the gatekeeper, "Ishtar may enter, but see to it she obeys the ancient laws."

The gatekeeper returned to the gate and said to Ishtar, "You may enter, Lady Ishtar. Enter and let the Underworld rejoice at your arrival."

The gatekeeper took Ishtar to the first gate. There he took from Ishtar her great crown and opened for her the gate.

"Why do you take from me my crown?" said Ishtar.

"I bid you enter, my lady," said the gatekeeper. "I take the crown because it is an ancient law of this place, and I must uphold it."

The gatekeeper took Ishtar to the second gate. There he took from Ishtar her earrings.

"Why do you take from me my earrings?" said Ishtar.

"I bid you enter, my lady," said the gatekeeper. "I take the earrings because it is an ancient law of this place, and I must uphold it."

The gatekeeper took Ishtar to the third gate. There he took from Ishtar her necklace of beads.

"Why do you take from me my necklace of beads?" said Ishtar.

"I bid you enter, my lady," said the gatekeeper. "I take the necklace of beads because it is an ancient law of this place, and I must uphold it."

The gatekeeper took Ishtar to the fourth gate. There he took from Ishtar the fastenings of her garment.

"Why do you take from me the fastenings of my garment?" said Ishtar

"I bid you enter, my lady," said the gatekeeper. "I take the fastenings of your garment because it is an ancient law of this place, and I must uphold it."

The gatekeeper took Ishtar to the fifth gate. There he took from Ishtar the belt decked with birthstones.

"Why do you take from me my belt decked with birthstones?" said Ishtar.

"I bid you enter, my lady," said the gatekeeper. "I take the belt decked with birthstones because it is an ancient law of this place, and I must uphold it."

The gatekeeper took Ishtar to the sixth gate. There he took from Ishtar the bracelets from her wrists and the anklets from her feet.

"Why do you take from me my bracelets from my wrists and the anklets from my feet?" said Ishtar.

"I bid you enter, my lady," said the gatekeeper. "I take the bracelets from your wrists and the anklets from your feet because it is an ancient law of this place, and I must uphold it."

The gatekeeper took Ishtar to the seventh gate. There he took from Ishtar the garment of her body.

"Why do you take from me the garment of my body?" said Ishtar.

"I bid you enter, my lady," said the gatekeeper. "I take the garment of your body because it is an ancient law of this place, and I must uphold it."

Ishtar entered the presence of Ereshkigal, who trembled with anger. Not waiting for Ereshkigal to speak, Ishtar approached her.

Ereshkigal cried out, "Namtar, my wise counsellor! Take Ishtar away from me at once! Let her be riddled with diseases of all kinds, diseases of her eyes and skin, diseases of her hands and feet, diseases of her heart and head. Take her away, and strike her thus!"

And so it was that Ishtar was held in the Underworld, cursed by Ereshkigal. And upon the earth, the bull would not mount the cow. The young groom did not lie down with his bride. The husband slept in one room, and the wife in another.

Papsukkal, the wise counsellor of the Annunaki, saw what happened upon the Earth, and he was greatly saddened. He cast himself into mourning, donning ragged garments and letting his hair go unkempt. In mourning, Papsukkal went before Ea and said, "The Lady Ishtar has gone into the Underworld, and all is awry. The bull will not mount the cow. The young groom will not lie with his bride. The husband sleeps in one room, and the wife in another."

Ea heard the words of Papsukkal and saw his grief. Ea therefore created Asushunamir, a eunuch of great beauty. Ea said to Asushunamir, "Go down to the Underworld. Go to the Lady Ereshkigal. She will be entranced by you. When her anger is appeased, ask her to swear by the Annunaki, and then ask her to give you the waterskin that you might drink."

Asushunamir did as Ea instructed, but when he asked for the waterskin, Ereshkigal became enraged. "How dare you ask this thing! You have no right. A curse be upon you! You shall beg crusts from the bakers of the city, and drink from the public sewer. You shall stand only in the shadows, and you shall dwell only within doorways. Drunk and sober alike shall strike you in the face."

Then Ereshkigal said to Namtar, "Go to the E-galgina, the Eternal Palace. Decorate the doorways with coral and fine shells. Bring forth the Annunaki, let them be seated upon golden thrones. Take up the Water of Life, and sprinkle it upon Ishtar. Then take her away from here, out of the Underworld."

Namtar did as Ereshkigal commanded. He decorated the doorways of the E-galgina with coral and fine shells. He brought forth the Annunaki and seated them upon golden thrones. He took up the Water of Life and sprinkled it upon Ishtar. Then he brought her to the gates.

At the first gate, he returned to Ishtar the garment of her body and let her out the gate.

At the second gate, he returned to Ishtar the bracelets of her wrists and the anklets of her feet and let her out the gate.

At the third gate, he returned to Ishtar the belt of birthstones and let her out the gate.

At the fourth gate, he returned to Ishtar the fastenings of her garment and let her out the gate.

At the fifth gate, he returned to Ishtar her necklace of beads and let her out the gate.

At the sixth gate, he returned to Ishtar her earrings and let her out the gate.

At the seventh gate, he returned to Ishtar her great crown and let her out the gate.

Ereshkigal also said to Namtar, "If Ishtar does not pay her ransom price, you are to return her to the Underworld. When you let her go, bring here Tammuz, her lover. Bathe him in clearest water, and anoint him with fragrant oil. Dress him in fine red clothing, and give him a flute of lapis to play music upon and a ring of carnelian to adorn his finger. Send prostitutes to him that he might delight in them."

Ishtar rose up from the Underworld and found Tammuz at his ease, playing music on his flute and delighting in prostitutes. "What is this that you do?" she said. "Why do you not hold yourself in mourning, seeing that I was held captive in the Underworld?"

Then Ishtar cursed Tammuz, saying, "May the Lady Ereshkigal take you in my stead!"

Belili, the sister of Tammuz, was adorning herself with jewelry when the wail for Tammuz went up. She cast aside her jewels and cried out, "Do not take from me my brother! On the day when Tammuz returns, the lapis flute and carnelian ring will rejoice. Those who wail and keen will rejoice, and the dead shall smell the incense."

Nergal and Ereshkigal

Two versions of this myth exist. The earlier version, which was found in Tell el-Amarna, Egypt, appears to date from the 15th or 14th centuries BCE. This version is relatively short and involves the god Nergal's hostile takeover of the Underworld with the help of a company of demons. One important function of this version of the text seems to have been to help ancient Egyptian scribes learn Akkadian.

In the longer, later, Babylonian version, Nergal receives special instructions from Ea about how to behave so as not to become captive in the Underworld, including the command not to give in to any desire he may have for Ereshkigal, the goddess of the Underworld, no matter how she might tempt him. Of course, Nergal follows all of Ea's commandments except the one about desire, and he eventually assumes the throne of the Underworld by becoming Ereshkigal's lover. It is the second, longer version that is presented here, although the ending has sadly been lost.

There came a time when the gods decided to hold a great feast, and so they sent a messenger to the Underworld to the goddess Ereshkigal, where she dwelled in her domain. The messenger said to Ereshkigal, "The gods, my masters, bid me to tell you that they are having a great feast. You cannot go up to their domain, and they may not come down to yours, so send a servant up to the gods so that the servant might bring you your share of the feast."

Ereshkigal called to herself her chief counsellor, Namtar. "Go up to where the gods are having their feast," said Ereshkigal. "Greet my fellow gods well, and bring back to me my portion."

Namtar went to the dwelling of the gods where they sat at their feast. When Namtar entered the banqueting chamber, the gods rose to greet him. One god, however, remained seated: Nergal. He refused to do honor to the chief counsellor of the goddess of the Underworld.

When Namtar returned to the Underworld with Ereshkigal's portion of the feast, he told her what had happened and how Nergal had refused to stand to honor him as the messenger of the goddess. Ereshkigal was greatly affronted. "Go back to the domain of the gods. Go thither, and bring back to me the one who did not honor you that I may kill him!"

Namtar went back to the domain of the gods. He said to them, "When I came to get Ereshkigal's portion of the feast, there was one among you who did not stand to greet me. I am commanded to bring him back with me so that he might answer for his insolence."

Namtar looked all around the hall, but he did not see Nergal among the other gods, for Nergal was greatly afraid, and he had crouched down behind the others so that Namtar might not see him.

Then Namtar went back to Ereshkigal and said, "I went to the domain of the gods. I looked for the one who slighted me, but he was not there."

"Go back to the domain of the gods," said Ereshkigal, "and ask the help of our father Ea. Tell him that the one who did not rise to greet you must come to my domain to answer for his insolence."

And so a third time Namtar returned to the domain of the gods. He went before Ea and said, "Ereshkigal, my mistress, demands that you send the one who slighted me to the Underworld that he might pay for his insolence."

Ea agreed and then sent Namtar back to the Underworld to give Ereshkigal his word that Nergal would be sent. Then Ea caused Nergal to come before him. Nergal was greatly frightened, for he knew why Namtar had been sent.

"O Father Ea!" pleaded Nergal. "Do not send me away. Do not send me to the Underworld, for surely Ereshkigal will kill me!"

"Have no fear," said Ea. "You will be safe if you do as I instruct you. Make for yourself a chair. Bring it with you to the Underworld. When the people of the Underworld offer you a seat, do not take it. Sit in your own seat instead. If they offer you food or drink, you must refuse it. And if Ereshkigal should show you her body, you must refuse that as well."

Nergal took up his axe. He went and cut down trees to make his chair. He fashioned the chair well and decorated it brightly. This done, he set out for the Underworld.

After a long journey, he came to the gates of Ereshkigal's domain. Nergal knocked on the gates. A guardian looked through the peephole and said, "Who are you, and what is your errand here?"

"I am Nergal, and I am come in answer to Ereshkigal's summons."

"Wait here," said the guardian. "I must ask whether I am to allow you to enter."

The guardian went to fetch Namtar. "There is a god at the gate. He says he has come in answer to the Lady Ereshkigal's summons."

Namtar went to the gate. He looked through the peephole, and when he beheld Nergal standing there, waiting, he began shaking with rage. Namtar went to Ereshkigal and said, "The god who slighted me is here at the gate. What should be done with him?"

"It is not for you to deal out judgment to him," said Ereshkigal. "Bring him into my presence. I shall deal with him as I see fit."

Namtar went back to the gate and let Nergal in. Namtar led Nergal through all the seven gates of the Underworld, one by one, until they came to the courtyard of Ereshkigal. There Nergal threw himself at the feet of the goddess. "Our father Anu sent me to your realm" he said. "I am here and will do your bidding."

"Sit down on this throne," said Ereshkigal. "Sit down here on my throne and pronounce judgment."

But Namtar remembered the instructions of Ea, and he did not sit on Ereshkigal's throne. He sat on his own chair instead.

Ereshkigal commanded her servants to bring food and drink to her guest. The food and drink were set before Nergal, but he remembered the instructions of Ea, and he did not touch it.

Then Ereshkigal said, "It is time for me to go and bathe." She went to her bath, and she made sure that Nergal could see her as she removed her clothing. She made sure that Nergal could see her body.

When Nergal beheld how beautiful Ereshkigal was and how comely her body, he was overcome with desire for her. He went to her and embraced her. Together they went to her bed where they delighted in one another as men and women do. There they lay together for six days, delighting in one another.

On the seventh day, Nergal rose from Ereshkigal's bed. "I must leave you now," said Nergal, "but have no fear. I shall return to you."

Nergal went to the guardian of the gate, saying, "You must let me out! The goddess Ereshkigal has said that I am to be allowed to return to the domain of the gods."

The guardian let Nergal out. Nergal ascended to the domain of the gods. The gods saw him return and said, "Lo! Nergal has come back! Let Ea bless him with fresh water, and let him sit once more among us and eat our food and drink our drink." And so it was that Nergal rejoined the company of the gods in their domain, blinking at the drops of fresh water that Ea had sprinkled upon him.

Ereshkigal, for her part, did not know that Nergal had left the Underworld entirely. She called to her servants to sprinkle fresh water for him and to set out food and drink for him. But then Namtar came into her chamber, saying, "Nergal is not here! He has left the Underworld entirely and has returned to the domain of the gods!"

Ereshkigal cried out in despair. "Alas!" she cried. "Alas that Nergal has left me! My bed shall be cold. My nights shall be empty. Never again shall I know delight. Alas!"

Namtar said to Ereshkigal, "Let me return to the domain of the gods. Let me ask Anu and Ellil and Ea to let Nergal return to you."

"Yes, my wise counsellor," said Ereshkigal. "Yes, go back to the domain of the gods. Tell Anu and Ellil and Ea that they must return

Nergal to me. I feel a stirring in my belly; surely he has left me with child. Also, you must tell them that if Nergal is not returned to me, I shall raise all the dead. I shall raise the dead, and send them into the land of the living. The dead shall eat the living, and no one shall be left alive!"

Namtar went up to the domain of the gods. He went before Anu and Ellil and Ea, and told them what the goddess said. "Ereshkigal demands you return her lover to her. He has left her with child. She weeps over her cold and empty bed. She desires him to return. If he does not return, Ereshkigal shall raise the dead, and the dead shall eat the living until no one is left alive."

"Very well," said Ea. "Search for the one you want. See whether he is here among us."

Nergal went through the company of the gods. He looked this one in the face and that one, and when he came to a god whose head had been sprinkled with water, he did not recognize that it was Nergal.

Namtar therefore returned to the Underworld, and told Ereshkigal what had happened. "I went to the domain of the gods. I gave your message to Anu and Ellil and Ea. I looked through all the company of the gods, but I did not see the one you desired. I looked through all of them, even the one who was blinking from the water that had been sprinkled on his head."

"That is the one!" said Ereshkigal. "The one with the water on his head is the one I desire. Go back to the domain of the gods, and tell them they must send that one to me."

Namtar returned to the domain of the gods. Once again he went through their company, seeking the one he was to take back to Ereshkigal. Finally he found Nergal. Namtar said to him, "You must come back with me to the Underworld. Ereshkigal desires you and wishes you to come and live with her in her domain."

"Very well," said Nergal. "I shall come with you."

Then Namtar said, "Listen well to my instructions. At each gate, you must give something that belongs to you to the guardian who is there. But do not let the guardian take hold of you."

While Namtar went back to Ereshkigal's domain, Nergal made himself ready. He thought about the words of Namtar. He took up his bow and his arrows, and descended to the Underworld. When Nergal arrived at the first gate, he commanded the guardian to let him in. The guardian opened the gate, but before he could demand one of Nergal's belongings from him, before the guardian could take hold of Nergal, Nergal struck him down. Nergal went to the second gate, and there he struck down the guardian. Nergal went to the third gate and the fourth, and at each gate to the Underworld, he struck down the guardian.

Finally, Nergal arrived at the courtyard where Ereshkigal was. He ran up to her where she was seated on her throne. He took hold of her long hair and pulled her into an embrace. Passionately they embraced, and then they went to Ereshkigal's bed, where they delighted in one another once more. There they lay for the first day and the second day. They lay for the third, the fourth, the fifth, and the sixth day. And on the seventh day, Anu sent his messenger to Ereshkigal and Nergal, where they dwelled in the domain of the Underworld.

[*The remainder of the story has been lost.*]

Ninurta and the Anzu Bird

The Anzu Bird is a mythical creature that appears in both Sumerian and Akkadian stories. Having the head of a lion and the body of a bird, this fearsome beast was associated with thunder and could be either a good or an evil character depending on the story.

It is the evil character that comes to the fore in this story: the Anzu Bird is made guardian of the dwelling of the gods, and when he sees the Tablets of Destiny that are kept by Ellil, he is overcome with greed and lust for the power that the tablets represent. One day, when Ellil is taking a bath, the Anzu Bird steals the tablets and runs away to the mountains with them, throwing the universe into chaos because the seat of authority has been removed from Ellil and given to the capricious bird. When the Anzu Bird (or more simply, "Anzu") refuses to give the tablets back, the gods send the hero Ninurta to recover them. In a series of battles involving both martial skill and magic, Ninurta finally recovers the tablets and restores them to their rightful owner, which also restores order to the cosmos.

Ninurta himself is a god, the son of Ellil and the mother goddess Ninhursag. Ninurta had associations with both agriculture and lawgiving, and in both Sumerian and Akkadian tales he is the one hero the gods themselves turn to when a powerful enemy presents itself and must be destroyed.

In the time when the great Tigris and Euphrates had been made, their channels dug so that they might flow through the land but before they had been filled with water, and in the time before any places of honor had been built for the Igigi, the Younger Gods of Heaven, the great god Ellil came before the Igigi and said, "Lo! Upon the mountain there has come to be a great bird, the Anzu Bird, whose beak is like a saw. I do not know where Anzu comes from. Perhaps he was born out of the Earth herself. Perhaps he was born out of the stone of the mountain itself. I say we should bring the Anzu Bird here, to serve us. Let him guard our holy of holies."

And so it was that Anzu was brought to the Duranki, the dwelling of the gods, to watch over the holy of holies. Every day, Ellil would go into the sacred chamber and there bathe himself with holy water, and Anzu would watch over him while he bathed. Anzu looked upon lordly Ellil, his fine clothes, and his golden crown, but most of all, Anzu gazed upon the Tablets of Destiny, which were in Ellil's keeping. Anzu looked upon the Tablets, and within his heart formed a great desire to have them for himself.

"Oh, if only I could be the holder of the Tablets!" Anzu said to himself. "Then I would be first among all the gods. All would have to bow to me. All the Igigi would be in my thrall. Surely the Tablets shall be mine!"

Anzu waited until the next time Ellil went to the holy of holies to bathe in the sacred water. When Ellil had set aside his golden crown and his fine raiment, and when he had set aside the Tablets of Destiny and entered the sacred water, Anzu swooped down upon the Tablets. He took the Tablets of Destiny in his talons and flew away to the mountain where he had been born. Ellil watched Anzu take the Tablets. He watched Anzu fly away with the authority of the gods, leaving the dwelling of the Igigi without any of its power.

The gods gathered together to take counsel of one another as to what should be done. Soon enough it was decided that someone should climb the mountain, kill Anzu, and bring the Tablets back to their rightful owners.

First the gods turned to Adad, the son of Anu. "Go and kill Anzu," said the other gods. "You are strong and a brave warrior. You are the god of storms and rain. You control the water in the canals. You will have holy places throughout the world, and everyone will praise your name if you do this deed."

But Adad said, "The mountain is impassable. No one can climb it. Anzu has the Tablets of Destiny. All authority and power rests in him now. Surely if I try to take the Tablets away from him, he will destroy me. No, I shall not go. Find another to do this deed."

Then the Igigi turned to Erra, the son of Annunitum, and asked him to go kill Anzu and bring back the Tablets. But Erra gave the same answer as Adad; he would not go.

Next, the Igigi asked Shara, the son of Ishtar. "Go climb the mountain and kill Anzu," they said. "You are strong and a brave warrior. You are the god of war and the son of the goddess Ishtar.

You will have holy places throughout the world, and everyone will praise your name if you do this deed. Bring back the Tablets!"

But Shara gave the same answer as Adad and Erra. He would not go.

The gods grew vexed. They argued with one another. They blamed each other that no one would go climb the mountain. No one would kill the Anzu Bird and take back the Tablets. Everyone was too afraid of Anzu's power.

Ea stood aside from the other gods and their wrangling. He thought long and deep, and then he went to his father, Anu, and said, "Let me be the one to find a champion. Surely I can find someone who will go to the mountain to face Anzu and bring back the Tablets."

Anu thought this a good plan, and when Ea told the Igigi what he had in mind, they praised him loudly.

First, Ea had the gods summon to themselves the goddess Mami. They said to her, "O Divine Mistress, we have need of your aid. We need you to give us your beloved son, the strong and bold Ninurta, for surely only he can deliver us from our plight. We beg you to ask his help."

Mami went to her son and told him what Ea and the Igigi had said. "You must go to the mountain and kill Anzu. You must bring back the Tablets of Destiny. The halls of the gods have lost their luster, and there is no power or authority here anymore. Go climb the mountain. Take your mighty bow, and pierce him with arrows. Surround him with mists and fog so that he cannot see you. Shine as brightly as the sun so that he is blinded by you. Kill Anzu, and bring back the Tablets, and you shall have shrines built to you throughout the whole world."

Ninurta heeded the words of his mother. He armed himself and set out for the mountain. When Anzu saw Ninurta approaching, he became very angry. "How dare you come to face me? How dare you threaten the bearer of the Tablets of Destiny? I am now the authority! Mine is the power of the gods! Away with you!"

Ninurta answered, "I am Ninurta! I have come from the sacred Duranki, sent by the gods themselves. I have come to kill you and take back that which you have unlawfully stolen. Have at you, foul demon!"

Anzu raged at Ninurta's words. He covered the whole mountain with darkness. Shrieking, he descended upon the brave Ninurta, and together they battled up and down the mountainside. Long and hard they fought, and in the end, Ninurta's armor was all splashed with blood, but the Anzu Bird did not die.

Ninurta took his mighty bow and nocked an arrow to the string. He set the arrow in flight, aiming it at Anzu's heart. Anzu saw the arrow and said to it, "Arrow shaft! Return your cane to its riverside. Fletching! Return your feathers to their birds. Bow! Return your wood to its forest. String! Return your gut to its sheep."

And so it was that Ninurta's arrow could not approach Anzu. The arrow turned away and did the bird no harm, and no matter how Ninurta might try, he could not get the bow to draw with any power. The Anzu Bird had bewitched that mighty weapon, and it was of no aid to Ninurta now.

Ninurta called out for help. He called to the god Adad and said, "O Adad! Go you to our father Ea and tell him that I cannot kill the Anzu Bird. We fought, but I could not defeat him, and he has bewitched my mighty bow and my swift arrows so that they are of no help to me. Tell this to Ea, and then bring his answer back to me."

Adad did as Ninurta asked. He went to Ea and told of all that had happened on the mountain, of how Ninurta had not been able to kill the bird, and of how Anzu had enchanted Ninurta's bow and arrows.

Ea replied, "My son, do not be afraid! Do not cease in your efforts! You will be victorious. Attack the Anzu Bird. Attack him relentlessly. Attack him until he tires and can fight you no more. Fight him until all the feathers drop from his wings, and then cut them off with your sword. Anzu will try to reattach his wings, but never fear; once his feathers and wings are lost, he will not be able to withstand you. Call up the winds; bid them blow his feathers and wings away. Then you may take your mighty bow and launch a swift arrow at his breast. Grab Anzu by the neck, take your sword, and slit open his gullet!

"Do these things, and do them well. Return the Tablets of Destiny to their rightful owners. Restore order. Do these things, and you shall have many shrines and much honor, in heaven and on the Earth."

Adad returned to Ninurta and told him everything Ea had said. Ninurta hearkened well and girded himself once more for battle. He took up his mighty sword, the Seven of Battle. He called to himself the seven winds, they who create the dust storms. The winds he called to himself to be his army, and he arrayed them for war.

Again Ninurta advanced upon the Anzu Bird. Again their battle was fierce. But Ninurta did not cease to press his attack. On and on, he harried the great bird. On and on, Ninurta pressed him until Anzu began shedding the feathers of his wings in his weariness. When Ninurta saw this, he drew his sword and slashed off Anzu's wings. Anzu tried to reattach his wings. "Wing to wing!" he shouted, but before he could complete the spell, Ninurta nocked a swift arrow to his mighty bow and sent the dart deep into the breast of the Anzu Bird.

Ninurta did not cease his fighting once the bird was dead. First he went and slew the mountain. Ninurta slew the mountain that the Anzu Bird had defiled. Then he flooded the plains all around. With that done, Ninurta took up the Tablets of Destiny that Anzu had stolen and set out for the abode of the gods.

While Ninurta was still journeying back, an omen came to the Igigi. A great number of feathers floated into the abode of the gods, the feathers of the Anzu Bird. Dagan, god of the growing grain, saw the feathers. He called to all the other gods, saying, "Rejoice! Surely the hero Ninurta has slain the Anzu Bird and taken back the Tablets of

Destiny. See? Here are the feathers of the great bird, floating into our abode on the wind. Rejoice!"

Soon enough, the brave Ninurta returned, bearing the Tablets of Destiny in his powerful arms. Ninurta placed the tablets in the lap of Ellil, restoring them to their rightful owner, restoring order to all that is.

Ellil said, "Behold! The hero Ninurta has slain the Anzu Bird and restored the Tablets of Destiny! Let us praise his name henceforth, in heaven and upon the Earth. May he have many shrines and be called by many holy names. Praise to the hero Ninurta!"

Adapa and the South Wind

This brief story may appear relatively simple at first glance, but it contains a great deal of depth and complexity. The tale of Adapa is at once a trickster story, a tale of the relationship between mankind and divinity, a story about the fatal refusal of immortality made by a man who was supposedly divinely wise (or who perhaps wisely refused immortality), and a just-so fable about why human beings are both mortal and separated from the gods. Some scholars have seen antecedents for the Genesis tale of Adam and Eve in the Garden of Eden within the myth of Adapa, in that the gods make eternal life available to the protagonist(s), who ultimately do not achieve it.

However, the roles of food and obedience in the eventual outcome of each of these stories are different. In both stories, the main characters are told by a divine being not to eat what is made available to them. Adapa obeys the command of Ea not to eat the food of the gods, while Adam and Eve disobey and eat the forbidden fruit. Adapa is later chastised by the great god Anu for failing to eat the food of life, but Adam and Eve are exiled from paradise for taking the forbidden fruit.

Once there was a man named Adapa, who was favored of the gods and who was the son of the god Ea. The gods gave him great wisdom, wisdom like unto their own wisdom, but to Adapa, they did not grant eternal life.

Adapa lived in the city of Eridu, and to him Ea gave authority over all things so that he might pronounce judgment upon the people. A wise man was Adapa, and a pious one. He served in the temple, baking the sacred loaves, catching the sacred fish. Adapa it was who opened the temple doors, and Adapa it was who closed them again.

One day, Adapa went down to the harbor, for there was need of fish to feed the gods. Adapa went to the dock where his little fishing boat was moored. He got into the boat, and away he sailed. With the power given to him by the gods, he steered his boat out onto the open water, where he laid his nets for a catch of fish.

Having caught enough fish, Adapa made ready to return to the harbor. The sea had been calm and unruffled the whole day. Adapa's sailing and fishing had been easy and very pleasant. But when he tried to sail back to the harbor, the South Wind flew down upon him. So great was the power of the wind that Adapa's little boat was capsized, and all his catch was lost.

This made Adapa very angry. "May your wing break!" he said to the South Wind, and as soon as he said it, the South Wind's wing was broken. The South Wind could not blow from the sea onto the land. For seven days, there was no cooling wind from the sea. For seven days, the heat of the sun was not abated by a southerly sea breeze.

The god Anu suffered much from the heat. He called to himself Ilabrat, his messenger. "Tell me, Ilabrat," said Anu, "why is it that there is no good breeze from the sea? Where are the cooling winds?"

"O Anu," said Ilabrat, "it is because the man Adapa has broken the South Wind's wing. It cannot fly to bring the coolness from the sea onto the land."

"Oh!" cried Anu. "Oh, this is a great insult. Bring the man Adapa before me to answer for what he has done!"

Ea heard of Anu's anger toward Adapa. Ea went to his son and said, "You will be summoned before the god Anu for breaking the South Wind's wing. Dress yourself in ragged clothes. Leave your hair uncombed. Behave as though you are in deep mourning.

"When you arrive at the door to Anu's house, there will be two gods waiting there for you. These are Tammuz and Gizzida. They will ask you why you were mourning. You must tell them that you are mourning for two gods who have vanished. They will ask you which gods, and you must tell them 'Tammuz and Gizzida.' Then they will laugh in mirth at this, and bring you into Anu's presence. There they will speak a good word for you.

"Tammuz and Gizzida may offer you the food of death and the drink of death. Do not eat it! Do not drink it! But if they offer you clean clothing and oil to anoint your body, put on the clothing and anoint yourself with the oil. Do not forget what I have told you!"

Adapa did what Ea told him. He dressed himself in ragged clothes. He left his hair unkempt. He put on an air of mourning. And in this guise, he went to the gates of the house of Anu, where Tammuz and Gizzida were waiting outside the door.

When the two gods saw Adapa, they said, "Adapa! Whatever is the matter? Why do you go about in rags with your hair unkempt and an air of mourning about you?"

"Oh," said Adapa, "it is very sad indeed. Two gods have vanished! They have vanished and will never return, so I am mourning for them."

"Which gods are these?" asked Tammuz and Gizzida.

"Why, Tammuz and Gizzida, of course," replied Adapa. "They have vanished quite away. It is very sad."

Tammuz and Gizzida looked at one another and then began to laugh. They laughed for a very long time. But when they could catch their breaths again, they brought Adapa into the house of Anu to stand before Anu himself.

Anu said to Adapa, "Tell me, why did you break the South Wind's wing?"

Adapa said, "O Great Anu, I went fishing on the sea to get fish to feed the gods. When I had enough fish, I wanted to sail back to the harbor, but the South Wind flew down upon me and capsized my little boat. I lost all my catch. This made me very angry, so I cursed the South Wind, and now its wing is broken."

Anu began to be very angry indeed with Adapa, but Tammuz and Gizzida spoke on Adapa's behalf. They calmed the anger of Anu, just as Ea had said they would.

Anu sighed. "What did Ea think to accomplish by giving such power to a mere mortal? What should we do with this Adapa?"

Anu turned to his servants. "Bring this man the food of life. Bring this man the water of life. Bring him fresh clothing and oil with which to anoint himself."

The food and drink and clothing and oil were given to Adapa. Adapa put on the garment and anointed himself with the oil, but he did not touch either the food or the drink.

Anu wondered that Adapa would not eat or drink. "Adapa, surely you are hungry and thirsty. Why do you not eat? Why do you not drink? Do you not wish to live?"

"O Great Anu," said Adapa, "my father Ea told me, 'When you go to the house of Anu, you must not eat the food. You must not drink the water.' That is why I do not eat or drink."

Anu laughed. "Very well, suit yourself! Surely it is a strange thing that Ea should tell a mere mortal to disobey the commands of Anu."

Anu caused Adapa to be returned to his home in Eridu, where he became even more renowned for his wisdom and piety. But because Adapa had refused the food and water of life, he did not live forever. Only the memory of his wisdom and piety lived on, for Anu ordained it to be thus.

Part III: Selections from the *Epic of Gilgamesh*

The Epic of Gilgamesh *is one of the first tales of its kind ever recorded. It follows the friendship and adventures of Gilgamesh, king of Uruk, and his companion, Enkidu, a wild man created by the gods to curb Gilgamesh's excesses. These stories originated in Sumer as a loosely connected collection of tales about Gilgamesh and his friend, but the version presented below is based on the two most important later Akkadian versions: the Old Babylonian, which was compiled sometime around 1800 BCE, and the so-called Standard Version, which was compiled around 1200 BCE.*

The Akkadian versions of Gilgamesh's tale contain some of the same stories that the Sumerian version does, but they go far beyond the Sumerian version in terms of characterization. For example, the Akkadian versions of Gilgamesh *introduce Enkidu as a round character in his own right, explaining his backstory and telling how he and Gilgamesh came to be friends. Also enfolded into the Akkadian* Gilgamesh *is a version of the Sumerian Flood myth as told* to Gilgamesh by Utnapishtim, the man who built the ark and survived that deluge and who was granted eternal life by the gods.

But above all, the Babylonian Gilgamesh is a meditation on friendship and mortality, showing the love that Gilgamesh and Enkidu have for one another and the extended journey Gilgamesh undertakes after his friend's death to find the secret of eternal life. Of course, every effort Gilgamesh makes in his attempt to gain immortality is doomed to failure, but at the end of the epic, he returns to his city of Uruk, apparently content that what he has achieved there as king should be his lasting legacy after his death.

Although in both the Akkadian epic and the Sumerian tales Gilgamesh is a semi-divine being and superhuman hero, he is based on an actual human ruler. The historical Gilgamesh ruled the city-state of Uruk sometime between 2800 and 2500 BCE. Legends about the mythologized Gilgamesh begin to appear in Sumerian some four to five hundred years later. The story was then lost for about three thousand years; the modern rediscovery of the tale happened in 1853, when Austen Henry Layard, Hormuzd Rassam, and W. K. Loftus found the tablets in the remains of the Royal Library of Ashurbanipal in the ruins of Nineveh, capital of the Assyrian Empire, which is near modern-day Mosul, Iraq.

Gilgamesh and Enkidu

One of the most famous friendships in all of human storytelling is that between Gilgamesh and Enkidu. At the beginning, Enkidu is a hairy wild man who knows nothing of human customs and who is sent by the gods to moderate Gilgamesh's excesses as king. Enkidu is civilized first by having sexual relations with a prostitute named Shamhat and then by being brought to a shepherd's camp where he is taught how to eat and drink as humans do and where his hair is shaven and shorn and he dons clothing as humans do. Enkidu goes to Uruk intending to challenge Gilgamesh and to put a stop to the king's practice of droit du seigneur, *which Enkidu finds abhorrent, but instead of killing Gilgamesh, he ends up becoming his best friend and companion in arms. Gilgamesh, for his part, is delighted to have finally found a companion who is truly his equal, and from that point on, the two are inseparable.*

Once there was a mighty king named Gilgamesh. His mother was a goddess and his father a great king. Enki himself shaped Gilgamesh's body, gave him his stature and his strength, his beauty of face, his thick wavy hair and beard, and all things that make a man beautiful to behold. No one could best Gilgamesh, either in sport or in battle, and he ruled as king over the city of Uruk as his father Lugalbanda had done before him, and his father's predecessor, the mighty Enmerkar, son of Utu the sun-god, before him.

Gilgamesh was mighty and the king of Uruk, but he did not rule either wisely or well. The young men he summoned to contest after contest, and would not let them go home to their mothers even after he had bested every one. When it came time for the young women to be wed, Gilgamesh took them for himself on their bride-night, only letting them go to their young husbands after he had had them.

The women of Uruk raised their voices to Anu, saying, "O great Anu, O mightiest among the gods, we pray your mercy on our behalf. This Gilgamesh rules us neither wisely nor well. He keeps our sons at his contests day and night, and never does he let them come home even after he has bested every one. And when our daughters are to be wed, he takes them for himself on their bride-night, not giving them to their rightful husbands until after he has had his way with them. O Anu, spare us! Save us from the rapacity of Gilgamesh!"

Anu saw the misdeeds of Gilgamesh, and he heard the cry of the women of Uruk. Anu said, "Let Aruru come forth. Let her create one who is the equal of Gilgamesh. Let him then be sent to Uruk to teach Gilgamesh a lesson!"

And so Aruru heeded the command of Anu. She took a piece of clay and threw it down upon the Earth. From the clay, she made Enkidu, and Ninurta granted to him his own strength. Enkidu had the form of a man, but he was all covered with long hair, and the tresses of his head hung unkempt over his shoulders and down his back. Enkidu knew neither mother nor father; the offspring of silence was he.

Enkidu lived in the wilds among the gazelles, and the gazelles accounted him as one of themselves. Together they ran and grazed and went to the waterhole to drink, and like the gazelles, Enkidu knew nothing of human speech or human customs.

One day, a hunter lay in wait near the watering hole, hoping to catch a gazelle. There he spied Enkidu coming down to the water with his herd. The hunter watched as Enkidu went around the watering hole, pulling up all the traps the hunter had laid to catch his prey. The hunter came back a second day and a third, and each was like the day before: Enkidu came to the watering hole and destroyed all the traps the hunter had laid.

Not knowing what else to do, the hunter went to his father and told him what he had seen. "Every day, this hairy, wild man comes down to the watering hole with the gazelles. He has the strength of a god, and every snare I set he destroys. I am afraid of him, and I do not know what to do."

The hunter's father said, "There is only one thing to do: go to Uruk, and tell King Gilgamesh what you have seen. Gilgamesh is the mightiest in the land; he will know what is to be done, and he will defeat this creature if that is what is needed."

The hunter took his father's advice and set out for Uruk the next morning. He went to the palace where he begged an audience of Gilgamesh. "O Gilgamesh, O mighty King of Uruk, I need your help. A hairy, wild man comes and destroys all the snares I set for game. Truly he has the strength of a god, and I am afraid of him. Please help me, for I have not been able to catch anything to feed my family for many days."

Gilgamesh said, "You must go back to the watering hole, but take the prostitute Shamhat with you. When the wild man appears, have her stand before him and remove her garments. Surely he will be entranced by her beauty and will wish to lie with her. Once he has done that, the herd will no longer account him as one of their own, and he will leave your snares alone."

The hunter did as Gilgamesh said. He went and asked Shamhat the prostitute to go with him, and she agreed, readily. Together the hunter and Shamhat went to the watering hole, and there they lay in wait for Enkidu and his herd. They waited one day, then two days, and on the third day, Enkidu and the gazelles appeared. Enkidu grazed with the herd and played in the water with them and moved about with them as though he were one of them. The hunter said, "There! There is the one I told you about, the hairy, wild man who lives with the gazelles! Go to him, reveal your body, and lie with him. Then maybe the herd will shun him, and I will be able to catch game again."

Then Shamhat came out of hiding and stood on the shore of the watering hole. When she was sure Enkidu was looking at her, she let her shift fall to the ground, revealing her naked body. Enkidu saw the beauty of Shamhat, and he greatly desired her. He went to her, and together they lay on the grass on top of her shift, which she laid out like a fine sheet on a beautiful bed. Enkidu lay in delight with Shamhat. For six days and seven nights they lay together, delighting in one another the whole time. When finally Enkidu's desire was sated, he went to rejoin his herd, but they no longer recognized him. They ran away from him, refusing to let him come near, and when Enkidu tried to run after them, he found that his legs had greatly weakened. He could no longer run among them as he used to do, for Shamhat had taken the wildness from him and replaced it with a man's reason.

So Enkidu went back to where Shamhat sat watching him. Enkidu sat at her feet, and she said to him, "Enkidu, you are as handsome as a god, and as strong. You shouldn't stay here among the beasts; you belong in the cities of men. I will take you back to my city, to Uruk, where Gilgamesh the mighty rules over all, and the temples of Anu and Ishtar rise above the plain in all their splendor."

Enkidu replied, "Yes, take me to your city! I desire to see its temples and to meet this Gilgamesh. There I shall challenge him, and we shall see which of us is mightiest."

"We will go to Uruk, and you shall taste of its delights. There are festivals with music and dancing, where the drummers and flute players play all day long. The prostitutes are so beautiful, none can withstand their charms. But put aside thoughts of challenging Gilgamesh; he is favored of the gods, and no man may best him, in sport or in battle."

In Uruk, Gilgamesh slept in his kingly bed, and he had a dream. It was a strange dream, and he did not know what it meant. So he went to his goddess-mother, the lady Ninsun, to see what she might make of it. "Mother, I have had the strangest dream. I would like to tell it to you to see what you will make of it."

"Tell me your dream, my son," said Ninsun, "and I will apply all my wisdom to it."

"In my dream, a great stone fell from the sky. It fell down into the center of Uruk, and there it sat. All the people gathered around it and wondered at it. I tried to lift the stone, but it was too heavy. I tried to roll the stone away, but I could not move it. And all the while, the people of Uruk gathered around the stone, praising it and kissing it.

"Then something changed. I found that I loved this great stone as a man loves his wife. I loved it as dearly as my own life. And when I loved the stone, I suddenly was able to move it. I picked up the stone and brought it back to you, Mother, where I laid it at your feet, and you said you would turn it into my equal. Tell me, what does this mean?"

"I think I see what this dream portends," said Ninsun. "There is one who is coming who you will love as a man loves his wife, who you will love as dearly as your own life. He will be your equal, and together you will have many adventures. He will save your life, and you will save his."

That night, Gilgamesh went to his rest, and again he had a dream. He dreamed of an axe that fell from the sky, and again all the people of Uruk gathered around it and praised it. Gilgamesh found that he loved the axe as he had loved the stone in the dream before, and just as in that dream, he picked up the axe and brought it to lay at Ninsun's feet.

In the morning, Gilgamesh asked his mother Ninsun what the dream foretold, and she said to him, "My son, this is like the dream of the stone. One is coming who you will love as dearly as your own life, and he will be your equal. He will save your life, and you will save his, and his strength will be like that of a god."

Hearing this, Gilgamesh rejoiced. "May Ellil make it so! I wish to have such a friend and such an equal. May it come true!"

Then it came time for Shamhat to take Enkidu away from the wild places that had been his home. She took her garment and rent it. Part of it she put on herself, and the other part she wrapped around Enkidu. Shamhat took Enkidu to an encampment of shepherds that lived nearby. When the shepherds saw Enkidu, they all gathered around him, wondering. "How like Gilgamesh he is, in stature and in build. This must be Enkidu, of whom we have already heard, for his strength is that of a god."

The shepherds invited Enkidu in and treated him as an honored guest. They set before him bread and good beer, but Enkidu had never seen these before and did not know what to do with them. Shamhat said to him, "Eat the bread, Enkidu! You need good food to keep you strong. Drink the beer! It is one of the delights of life."

And so Enkidu ate his fill and drank of the beer, seven whole goblets full. Soon he was feeling very merry and sang songs. When the meal was done, the barbers of the camp came to Enkidu. They shaved him and anointed him with oil. They shaved away all the beast from him;

they cut his locks and trimmed his beard and dressed him in warrior's garments, and thus it was that Enkidu became a man. Then Enkidu lived among the shepherds, chasing away wolves and lions, watching over the people and their flocks. And when Enkidu slept, he did so with Shamhat the prostitute, and they continued to delight in one another every night.

One night as Enkidu and Shamhat lay together, Enkidu happened to look up and saw a man standing not far away. He seemed to wish to speak to Enkidu, so Enkidu said to Shamhat, "Do you know that man? Do you know what he wants? Bring him here so that I may find out what he needs of me."

Shamhat brought him over, and Enkidu said, "Tell me, what is it you want? How may I aid you?"

The man said, "I was invited to a wedding banquet in Uruk. That is a time when a man takes a wife, and everyone celebrates. But in Uruk, the king demands that the young woman not spend her bride-night with her husband. Instead, Gilgamesh takes the woman back to his palace and has his way with her. Gilgamesh says that this is his right because he is king." And as the man spoke, his voice shook with anger.

Enkidu heard what the man said, and he became angry as well. He set out for Uruk that instant, and Shamhat went with him. When Enkidu entered the city, all the people looked at him in wonder. "Who can this be? He is just as tall as Gilgamesh and just as well made in his body. Surely this man has the strength of a god!"

Enkidu went to the place where the marriage feast was being held. He saw the marriage-house all arranged with a fine bed, a place to be blessed by the goddess of weddings. Then Enkidu saw Gilgamesh, a man like him in stature and build. Gilgamesh took the hand of a young woman dressed in fine linen and golden jewelry, and led her to the marriage-house. He ushered the young woman in, but before Gilgamesh could enter himself, Enkidu stood in the way and put his foot in the door. Gilgamesh was enraged at this presumption. He grappled with Enkidu, and combat was joined.

Up and down the town square they fought. They landed such blows that the doors shuddered in their jambs. They knocked one another down with such force that all the windows shuddered in their frames. Up and down the town square they fought, neither one able to get the best of the other. They fought as the day went from morning to afternoon and then as afternoon wore away to sunset, but neither one could claim himself the victor. Finally, they stood panting and glaring at one another, and Gilgamesh said, "You have done a thing that no other in the land has ever been able to do. You have fought with me up and down the town square, landing blows and knocking me down, and I have done the same to you, and yet neither of us is the victor. None before you has done this feat. Come, let us clasp hands and kiss one another, for I think we should be friends!"

Gilgamesh and the Bull of Heaven

In the story that precedes this one, Gilgamesh and Enkidu have gone to the Mountains of Cedar to slay the forest giant Humbaba. With that task accomplished, Gilgamesh and Enkidu arrive home safely only to find that another threat awaits them. The goddess Ishtar sees how beautiful and brave Gilgamesh is and proposes marriage to him, but when he refuses, she sends the Bull of Heaven down to destroy him. Of course, Gilgamesh and Enkidu manage to slay the Bull, but the combination of this deed and the slaying of Humbaba will prove fatal to Enkidu. The episode of the Bull of Heaven ends with Gilgamesh and Enkidu being welcomed to a banquet in their honor, but in the following story, we learn that the gods have looked unfavorably on Gilgamesh's exploits and declare that one of the two friends must die.

The story of the Bull of Heaven is one of those having a parallel in the Sumerian version of the epic. The basic plot of both versions is the same. Gilgamesh comes home from killing Humbaba (Sumerian Huwawa), and Ishtar (Sumerian Inanna) proposes marriage.

Gilgamesh refuses, and so Ishtar/Inanna, in a fit of temper, sends the Bull to destroy Gilgamesh and his city. In the Sumerian version, Gilgamesh attempts to placate Inanna by offering her treasure and animals from his flocks, while in the Akkadian version, Ishtar tries to get Gilgamesh to agree to her proposal by promising to enrich him and increase his political power. Gilgamesh's refusal in the Akkadian version also is much more forceful: he recites a litany of the fates of Ishtar's past lovers and states baldly that he refuses to become yet another male to first become her lover and then have the bad luck to fall afoul of her.

Gilgamesh came home to Uruk. He came home from his quest and found that his clothing, body, armor, and weapons were dusty and spattered with blood. Gilgamesh took off his dirty clothing, and he cleaned his armor and weapons. Then Gilgamesh cleaned himself well in the bath, washing all of the dirt of his adventure from his body and his hair and beard. He put on fresh, clean clothing. He combed out his hair and put on his crown.

Then the lady Ishtar saw Gilgamesh. She saw how well dressed he was, how well made he was in his body and how fair of face, and she desired him greatly. Ishtar went to Gilgamesh and said, "O Gilgamesh, come to me and be my bridegroom! Let us delight in one another, as husband and wife! Marry me, and I will give you riches beyond compare, a chariot made of gold and lapis lazuli, with lions to pull it for you. I will give you a house made with fragrant cedar, and when you arrive home, even the threshold and your throne shall kiss your feet. Kings and lords from all the lands around will honor you and bring you tribute. All your flocks will increase two- and three-fold, and your beasts of burden will never tire. Come to me! Marry me! Let us be husband and wife together!"

Gilgamesh replied, "Lady Ishtar, were you to give me all that and nothing else, still I would be in your debt. Never could I match those rich gifts. What happens to me when you no longer delight in my company, when you no longer wish to share my bed, when my body no longer sets yours aflame with desire?

"My lady, well I know what happens to those who accept your offers. Well I know what happens to lovers who give in to your charms. How many of those have there been now? How many have you loved and discarded? Perhaps we should count them together. There was Tammuz, who loved you first, but who now sits in the Underworld where he weeps in perpetuity. Next came the *allallu*-bird, but when he displeased you, you broke his wing, and now he sits in the forest crying for pain. After that, you loved the lion, and when you were through with him, you dug for him a pit, and when he fell in, you left him there. You loved the horse, but in return for his devotion, you gave him a whip and spurs to make him gallop endless miles, and for his reward at the end a pail of muddy water.

"Once you loved a shepherd. He toiled for you, baking fresh bread, slaughtering and cooking a lamb for you, every day. And his reward? To be turned into a wolf, driven away by his friends, chased down and bitten by the dogs. And after him was Ishullanu, the gardener. Every day, he brought you a basket full of dates. Him you looked upon with desire, saying, 'Come to my bed! Touch me in my private parts! Let me caress you, let us delight in one another,' but he refused you again and again, and only gave in because you would not relent. And when he pleased you no longer, you turned him into a frog, and now he sits lamenting in the middle of his withered garden, for he no longer is able to labor in it as he used to.

"Come, my lady," said Gilgamesh, "Why should I accept your offer, generous as it is, knowing what has happened to everyone who has loved you before? I doubt that even I would be able to escape such a fate, should I displease you."

Hearing Gilgamesh's words, Ishtar flew into a rage. She ran shrieking into heaven and went to her father Anu and mother Antu, tears streaming down her cheeks. "Mother! Father! Come to my aid! Gilgamesh has been saying terrible things about me! He heaps insult after insult upon me, and it is unbearable."

Anu said, "What did you say to him? Did you provoke him so that he spoke to you thus?"

Ishtar replied, "Father, give me the Bull of Heaven. Give it to me, and I shall send it to slay Gilgamesh and trample his palace into dust. And if you will not give me the Bull, then I shall destroy the Underworld. The dead I shall raise and set them upon the living to devour them until there are more dead than living upon the Earth."

"If I give you the Bull of Heaven," said Anu, "then famine shall descend upon Uruk, famine lasting seven years. What provision have you made for the people and their beasts? Have you set aside grain and chaff and hay for them?"

"Yes, I have grain and chaff and hay aplenty, enough for seven years," said Ishtar.

And so Anu gave to Ishtar the Bull of Heaven. Ishtar led the Bull down onto the Earth, and together they journeyed until they reached Uruk. When the Bull entered Uruk, the trees and the plants all withered and died. The waters of the Euphrates diminished, receding by seven full cubits. The Bull uttered a great snort, and a pit opened beneath the feet of the men of Uruk. A hundred men toppled into the pit. The Bull uttered a second snort, and another pit claimed two hundred men of Uruk. At its third snort, a pit opened at the feet of Enkidu, who fell in up to his waist.

Enkidu jumped out of the pit and grabbed the Bull by its horns. Enraged, the Bull spat in Enkidu's face. It lifted its tail and poured dung all over him.

Enkidu called to Gilgamesh for aid. "Come, my friend! We must defend our city and our people! I have tried myself against the Bull of Heaven, and I know its strength and what it can do, and I know how we might defeat it. I will grab hold of the beast's tail and brace my foot against the back of its leg. Then you must take your knife and slay it as butchers do cattle. Slide your knife into its neck behind the skull, and do it quickly while I hold its tail!"

Enkidu went behind the Bull and grabbed hold of its tail. He braced his foot against the back of its leg. Then Gilgamesh drew his knife and plunged it with skill and strength into the spot on its neck behind the skull, and the Bull fell down, dead. The two friends opened up the Bull's chest and pulled out its heart. They went to the temple and offered the heart to Shamash, bowing down before him. Then they went and sat together, side by side, like brothers.

When Ishtar saw that the Bull had been slain and its heart offered to Shamash, she shrieked in fury and climbed upon the walls of Uruk. "Woe to you, Gilgamesh! Woe to you for your insults and for killing the Bull of Heaven!"

Enkidu heard the shrieks of Ishtar. He pulled off one of the Bull's haunches and flung it toward her. "Here is your portion," he cried, "and if I could catch you, I would do the same to you, and wrap your arms in the guts of the Bull besides!"

Ishtar sent a summons throughout the city. She called together all the courtesans and prostitutes, and set them to mourning over the haunch of the Bull. Gilgamesh, meanwhile, called together the craftsmen of the city. They sawed off the Bull's horns, each weighing thirty *minas* of lapis lazuli. So great were they that they could hold six *kor* of oil.

Gilgamesh took the horns, hallowed them for the anointing of the god Lugalbanda, and filled them with holy oil, and when that was done, Gilgamesh hung the horns in his bedchamber. Then Enkidu and Gilgamesh went to the river to wash the sweat and dust and blood of battle from their bodies and clothing, and when they were refreshed, they returned to the palace in a chariot, where they stood hand in hand.

As they drove through the streets, the people of Uruk gathered to shout their praises. Gilgamesh asked the serving girls of his household, "Tell me, who is the most beautiful of all men, and who the bravest of all heroes?" And they replied, "Why, Gilgamesh is the most beautiful of all men and Enkidu the bravest of all heroes!"

Then Gilgamesh and Enkidu went into the palace where a great feast had been laid in their honor, and there they ate and drank and made merry long into the night.

The Wanderings of Gilgamesh

After killing the Bull of Heaven, Enkidu is cursed by the gods for his presumption. Enkidu falls ill, and after many days of suffering, he dies. Gilgamesh is heartbroken at the loss of his companion, and he becomes more aware than ever of death and of his own mortality. He wanders in the wilderness, looking for Utnapishtim, the man who survived the Great Flood, thinking to get from him the secret of eternal life. In the process, Gilgamesh becomes a wild man of a sort himself, living in the open, wearing animal skins for clothing, and hunting prey for his food. It is not until Gilgamesh encounters Utnapishtim and hears his story that Gilgamesh is restored to a more civilized state.

Having sung a lament for Enkidu and buried him with all ceremony as is fit and proper, Gilgamesh sat and wept. He wept not only for his dead friend but also for himself. "Enkidu, best of companions, is dead. He has gone into the Underworld. Never more will he see the light of the sun or taste of clear water or freshly baked bread. Never more will he be at my side through thick and thin, my strong, brave companion Enkidu. For he has died and gone down into the Underworld, as we all must go. Even I, Gilgamesh, King of Uruk, child of the gods, must one day die.

"I do not wish to die. Death is a fearsome thing. I am afraid of dying. I must find a way to cheat death, to escape that fate. I will go into the wild and look for Utnapishtim, for he of all human beings was made immortal by the gods. I shall find him and ask him how I might go about cheating death myself."

And so Gilgamesh went into the wilderness. When fierce beasts attacked him, Gilgamesh fought with them. He killed the beasts, skinned them, and roasted their flesh and ate it. Gilgamesh wandered long in the wilderness, clad in the pelts of lions and hyenas and gazelles, living on what game he could catch, always looking for the way to the abode of Utnapishtim.

Shamash, the sun-god, looked down upon Gilgamesh and grew worried. "Gilgamesh, what is this that you do to yourself? Why do you wander the wilderness, clad in the pelts of animals, ever wandering and never resting? You will never seek what you find."

Gilgamesh replied, "Why should I rest now? When I am dead, I shall rest forever. Why should I stop wandering now? At least now I can still see the light of the sun; in the Underworld, all is darkness and dust, forever. No, I will not stop. I will wander as I may; it is my will."

And so Gilgamesh continued to wander the world until he came to the towering mountain of Mashu, who crest meets the sky and whose roots went down into the bottom of the Underworld itself. Gilgamesh reached the gates to the mountain and found them guarded by two scorpion-beings, fearsome to behold and deadly. They shone with a radiance nearly as bright as Shamash himself, for it was their duty to guard him as he rose in the morning and set in the evening. Gilgamesh looked upon the scorpion-beings and fell to his knees. He covered his face in fear before them.

"Who is this who comes before us?" said one scorpion-being to the other. "Why is he here?"

The other replied, "I know who this is. This is Gilgamesh, King of Uruk, and the blood of the gods flows in his veins." Then the second scorpion-being looked upon Gilgamesh and said "You there, who kneels before us, why have you come to our mountain? What is it you seek here? Explain yourself!"

"I am looking for the abode of Utnapishtim," said Gilgamesh. "I have wandered the whole world looking for the way to his abode, for he has the secret of eternal life, and I wish to learn that of him for myself."

The first scorpion-being said, "Very well, we will tell you the way, for never has a mortal man ever found his way to our mountain gate. But be warned: the way you go is dark and lightless, for it is the path Shamash himself follows after he sets in the west at nightfall. Have you the courage to brave that darkness?"

"I have known nothing but darkness and grief since the death of my companion," said Gilgamesh. "What can this new darkness possibly add to that? Tell me the way."

"Very well," said the second scorpion-being. "You must go through these gates and down into the dark tunnel that lies beyond. On, on, on you must go in the darkness, and you must never stop until you reach the other side. Do not stop, no matter how fearful you are! Go on until you see the light of day again. Twelve hours is the journey on the path Shamash follows. Twelve hours must you also journey on, in total darkness."

Then the scorpion-beings opened wide the gates of their mountain, and Gilgamesh walked through them into the darkness that lay beyond. For one hour, Gilgamesh walked. The darkness around him was complete; he could see neither in front of him nor behind. For two hours, Gilgamesh walked, and three and four, and never a ray of light did he see. On and on, Gilgamesh walked, and as he walked, he could feel the great weight of the darkness pressing down upon him. A fifth hour, and a sixth, and a seventh he walked through the darkness, and never a ray of light did he see. An eighth hour he walked on, and he began to think that maybe he had entered the Underworld itself, that he was dead already and would never see the light of day again. But he summoned all his courage and walked on.

At the ninth hour, Gilgamesh found hope, for a cool breeze blew along the path. His strength renewed, Gilgamesh walked on for a tenth hour, and an eleventh, and at the end of the twelfth hour, he could see a glimmer of light ahead of him, the light of the morning sun. Gilgamesh rejoiced and ran toward the light. He ran out into this bright new place and found himself in the orchard of the gods, where fresh grapes grew on vines of cornelian, where trees of lapis lazuli bore fruit of their own that perfumed the entire orchard, and all sparkled in the light of the morning sun.

Gilgamesh walked through the orchard, looking about him in delight. When he came to the other side, there he found a tavern, which had been built on the shore of the sea. The owner of the tavern was a wise old woman named Siduri. She saw Gilgamesh approaching and knew him for one who had the blood of the gods in his veins. But he was clad all in the pelts of animals and had a fearsome, wild aspect, and so Siduri barred the door of the tavern so that Gilgamesh could not enter. Then Siduri went up onto the roof, the better to watch what Gilgamesh might do.

Gilgamesh saw the old woman bar the door of the tavern, and a few moments later, he saw her up on the roof, watching him. "Old woman," shouted Gilgamesh, "why do you bar your door to me? What have I done that you should fear me? Know this: if you do not open to me willingly, I shall break down your door myself!"

"I barred the door because I do not know who you are or why you are here," said Siduri. "Tell me of yourself, that I may judge whether it is wise to open to you."

"I am Gilgamesh, King of Uruk. My brave companion Enkidu and I slew the forest giant Humbaba. Together we slew the Bull of Heaven. Together we hunted lions in the mountains, and there we slew many."

"A likely story," said Siduri. "If you really are a king and a hero like you say, why is your face so gaunt and your hair so matted? Why do you go about dressed in dirty beast pelts? You certainly look nothing whatever like a king and certainly nothing like Gilgamesh, of whom I have heard."

"My face is gaunt and my hair is matted and I wear beast pelts because I have been wandering in the wilderness. I wander the wilderness because my brave companion Enkidu, who bore many dangers with me and who I loved most dearly, has died. He was cursed by the gods and has gone down into the Underworld to drink dust. After my friend died, I became afraid of death, and now I am seeking the abode of Utnapishtim, that I may ask of him the secret to eternal life.

"Can you tell me the way, O innkeeper? How may I find the abode of Utnapishtim? If I must cross the sea, I will do it. If I must cross the desert, I will do it. If I must climb a mountain, I will do it. Tell me the way, if you know it. And if you do not know it, I shall wander the wilderness until I find it for myself."

"This is a fool's errand you are on," replied Siduri. "No one has ever crossed that sea but Shamash himself. And even if you could make the crossing, it is so dangerous that you would never survive it. Even if you sail the sea, the Waters of Death are halfway between here and there and block the way forward. You cannot get to Utnapishtim without crossing them. What will you do then?

"But if cross you must, you must go to Urshanabi, the boatman of Utnapishtim. You will find him over yonder, with the stone-beings who are his companions and shipmates. You will find them in the pine forest, cutting down saplings to use for barge poles. Go to Urshanabi, and ask whether he will take you across. But if he will not take you, there will be no way across for you, and you must go back the way you came!"

Gilgamesh went into the pine forest where he saw Urshanabi at work with the stone-beings. Gilgamesh drew his axe and his dagger and then fell upon them. Urshanabi saw Gilgamesh coming and took up his own axe to defend himself and his companions, but he was no match for Gilgamesh. Gilgamesh knocked Urshanabi down, and he lay stunned on the ground. Then Gilgamesh attacked the stone-beings, shattering their bodies and throwing the pieces into the river that flowed through the forest.

When the stone-beings had all been slain, Gilgamesh went back to Urshanabi and stood over him. Urshanabi opened his eyes and saw Gilgamesh standing there. Gilgamesh said, "Tell me your name."

"I am Urshanabi, boatman to Utnapishtim. Who are you?"

"I am Gilgamesh, King of Uruk. My brave companion Enkidu and I slew the forest giant Humbaba. Together we slew the Bull of Heaven. Together we hunted lions in the mountains, and there we slew many. I took the path of Shamash under the mountains, and I am seeking the abode of Utnapishtim."

"A likely story," said Urshanabi. "If you really are a king and a hero like you say, why is your face so gaunt and your hair so matted? Why do you go about dressed in dirty beast pelts? You certainly look nothing whatever like a king and certainly nothing like Gilgamesh, of whom I have heard."

"My face is gaunt and my hair is matted and I wear beast pelts because I have been wandering in the wilderness. I wander the wilderness because my brave companion Enkidu, who bore many dangers with me and who I loved most dearly, has died. He was cursed by the gods and has gone down into the Underworld to drink dust. After my friend died, I became afraid of death, and now I am seeking the abode of Utnapishtim, that I may ask of him the secret to eternal life. Now, tell me how I may get there, for the innkeeper said that you know the way."

"I do know the way," said Urshanabi, "but you have taken from us the means to get there. I cannot manage the boat without the help of the stone-beings, nor without the barge poles they were making, and you have killed them all."

"Tell me what you need," said Gilgamesh, "and I will provide it."

"Cut down pine saplings, and strip them to use as barge poles. We will need 120. When the saplings are stripped, put a boss on the end of each of them."

Gilgamesh took his axe and cut down 120 saplings. Then he took his dagger and stripped them. When that was done, he put a boss on the end of each of them. Then Gilgamesh helped Urshanabi launch the boat into the sea. Together Gilgamesh and Urshanabi rowed the boat. Now, the journey from the shore to the Waters of Death normally would take two months, but with Gilgamesh's help, they arrived in only three days.

At the edge of the Waters of Death, Urshanabi said, "Take up a barge pole, Gilgamesh, and punt us across the waters. But take care not to touch the waters, for they will shrivel up your hand!"

Gilgamesh took up the first pole and began to punt them across the Waters of Death while Urshanabi steered. Soon the first barge pole was no longer of any use, so Gilgamesh took up the second. And when the second was no longer of any use, Gilgamesh took up the third, and the fourth, and the fifth. After he had punted them a long way but before they had arrived at the other side, Gilgamesh had used up all the poles.

"What will we do now?" said Urshanabi. "We have no more poles."

"Strip off your garments," said Gilgamesh. "I shall strip mine also, and we shall use them for a sail."

"But there is neither mast nor yardarm on this craft," said Urshanabi.

"I shall be both mast and yardarm," said Gilgamesh. And so Gilgamesh and Urshanabi stripped off their garments, and Gilgamesh stood up in the middle of the boat and held his arms open wide. Urshanabi took the garments and made of them a sail, hanging it from Gilgamesh's mighty arms while his body served for a mast, and in this way they sailed across to the place where Utnapishtim made his abode.

Now, Utnapishtim happened to look out over the water as Urshanabi and Gilgamesh were sailing toward him. Utnapishtim said to himself, "I see there Urshanabi, my boatman, but who is that with him? I do not recognize him at all."

Soon enough, Urshanabi and Gilgamesh arrived on the shore where they found Utnapishtim waiting for them.

"My boatman I know," said Untapishtim to Gilgamesh, "but who are you?"

"I am Gilgamesh, King of Uruk. My brave companion Enkidu and I slew the forest giant Humbaba. Together we slew the Bull of Heaven. Together we hunted lions in the mountains, and there we slew many. I took the path of Shamash under the mountains, and I sailed across the sea and across the Waters of Death, for I am seeking Utnapishtim."

"Utnapishtim you have found, for he stands here before you. But I do not believe your tale of yourself. If you really are a king and a hero like you say, why is your face so gaunt and your hair so matted? Why do you go about dressed in dirty beast pelts? You certainly look nothing whatever like a king and certainly nothing like Gilgamesh, of whom I have heard."

"My face is gaunt and my hair is matted and I wear beast pelts because I have been wandering in the wilderness. I wander the wilderness because my brave companion Enkidu, who bore many dangers with me and who I loved most dearly, has died. He was cursed by the gods and has gone down into the Underworld to drink dust. After my friend died, I became afraid of death, and that is why I have sought you out, that I may ask you the secret of eternal life."

"Oh, Gilgamesh," said Utnapishtim, "the blood of the gods runs in your veins, and yet you behave thus? You were given a throne and riches, and you have cast them all away in exchange for a life of endless toil in the wilderness and a fool's errand. Death comes for everyone in the end, and no one ever sees his face. Death creeps up on them and takes them unawares. We may build fine houses and bridges and boats, but nowhere may we hide from Death. Those he takes are gone forever, and we never see them again. This is the fate the Annunaki have decreed. Life they have given, but also death, and the gods may not be gainsaid."

Gilgamesh and Utnapishtim

This final chapter of the Epic of Gilgamesh *contains a retelling of the Sumerian flood myth by Utnapishtim, the builder of the ark and the only man ever to attain immortality. When Utnapishtim is done with his tale, Gilgamesh asks him how he might become immortal as well. Utnapishtim tells him that he must stay awake for six days and seven nights, whereupon the exhausted Gilgamesh promptly lies down and sleeps for that much time. Despairing of ever reaching his goal, Gilgamesh prepares to leave Utnapishtim, but the latter's wife reminds him that there is one other possible route for Gilgamesh to take: go to the bottom of the sea and find the plant of life. Gilgamesh succeeds in this, only to lose the plant to a thieving serpent when he is making the journey home to his own city.*

Gilgamesh and his companion Urshanabi travel together until they reach Uruk. Upon their arrival, Gilgamesh boasts to Urshanabi of the prosperity of Uruk and proposes a tour of the city walls. The epic ends here, with Gilgamesh safely returned home and proud of his accomplishments as the King of Uruk.

Gilgamesh stood on the shore and looked at Utnapishtim. Then he said, "At first I thought that you might be like a god and that I would need to fight you. But now that I see you, I understand that you are a man, just like me. Tell me, O eldest one, how is it that you came to be immortal? How might this gift be obtained? For I do not wish to die. I do not wish to go into the Underworld to drink dust."

"I will tell you this," said Utnapishtim, "even though it is a secret known only to the gods. Once I lived in the city of Shuruppak, a fine city on the banks of the Euphrates wherein even the gods dwelt once. The great god Anu had become angry with the people, and he resolved to send down a Great Flood to wash them all away. He took counsel of Ellil and Ninurta, and they agreed that this was a good plan. Even Ea, the most wise, took an oath that this thing should be done. But when Ea did so, he went near my house and whispered into the walls his oath to bring the Great Flood, and so I learned what it was the gods resolved to do.

"Ea also whispered to me that I should build a great boat and place therein every kind of living thing. He whispered to me how long the boat should be and how wide, and he told me to put a roof over it. I said to Ea, 'O mighty Ea, wisest of the wise, I hear your command, and I obey. But surely the elders of my city will notice the boat as I build it. What shall I say to them when they ask me what it is I do?'

"Ea said to me, 'Tell them that you have run afoul of Ellil and so can no longer live in the city. Tell them that I have given you the command to build the boat, that I am going to take you to live with me in my dwelling in the Apsu. Tell them that if they help you build the boat, I will shower upon them fresh bread and fresh fish, enough for a feast!'

"And so it was that I commenced building the boat. I hired workmen to fell the trees and mill the lumber, to construct the hull and put inside it the decks. After five days, the hull was complete. The boat measured ten rods high, and it covered a full acre of land. Six decks it had, and the inside was divided into nine compartments. Every day, I slaughtered lambs and oxen to feed my workers. I fed them well; every day was like a feast!

"When all was finished, I loaded the boat with all my goods and with food and water for people and beasts alike. I took aboard all of my family and also workmen who were skilled in their crafts. I took aboard the animals, as Ea had instructed me, wild beasts and tame alike. I took all these things aboard and waited for the sign Ea said would come, the shower of fresh bread and fresh fish, enough for a feast!

"Soon enough that sign came, and so I looked to the heavens to see what would happen next. I watched the sun rise, and as Shamash started his path across the sky, a great wall of black clouds rose up behind him, and within those clouds stormed Adad, the god of rain, and his attendants stormed along with him. The Annunaki came, too, and wherever they passed, they called down lightning that struck down trees and destroyed houses and breached the city walls. The river rose and began to overflow its banks, and still the storm wind of Adad continued to blow, and the rain came down.

"Then the whole world went black as night, and for a moment, it was still. And then came the Great Flood, a great surge of water that swept away all before it. It scoured the land clean of all living things and rose many rods above the tops of the highest trees. The water climbed up the sides of the mountains, covering all but the peaks of the very tallest.

"The gods looked down upon the flood they had unleashed, and they became frightened. They ran away to their abode in the heavens where they sat cowering like dogs. When the goddess Belet-ili saw what the gods had wrought, she wailed and lamented. 'Woe that I agreed to this course! Woe that I had a part in the destruction the flood has wrought! For all my children have been swept away, and now they float in the water like fish.'

"The Annunaki looked down at what they had wrought, and they quailed there in their abode in the heavens. They looked down on what they had wrought, and they wept for sorrow and for shame. But on and on the storm raged, for this is what the Annunaki had commanded. For six days and seven nights did it rain, for six days and seven nights did the winds blow a gale. And on the seventh day, the rain stopped, and the winds quieted, and the waves of the ocean that had been like very hills quieted, and my boat floated upon a calm sea under the light of Shamash.

"I opened one of the portholes in the side of the boat and saw the light of Shamash. I looked out, and everywhere I looked was nothing but sea, except for fourteen islands that had been the highest mountain peaks. I saw what had become of the world, and I wept bitter tears. We floated upon the waters for a while, but then the boat ran aground on Mount Nimush, and there we sat for six days. On the seventh day, I released a dove, to see what had become of the land, but the dove returned, for there was no place for her to perch. I did the same with a swallow, and it, too, came back. Then I brought out a raven and let it go, but it did not come back, for the waters had begun to recede, and it was able to find food.

"When the raven did not return, I sacrificed to the gods. I burned incense there on the top of the mountain, and the scent of it rose into the nostrils of the gods and pleased them. As the incense burned and the smoke of it arose, the goddess Belet-ili appeared and said, 'Surely this incense will draw all the gods nigh. But let Ellil stay away, for it was his counsel that the world should be destroyed by a Great Flood.'

"Just then, Ellil arrived. He saw the boat and the people and the animals who had survived the flood, and he was most wroth. 'How is it that these have survived? Who is it that told them to prepare, that they might be spared? Who is it that went against the will of the Annunaki?'

"Ninurta said, 'Who else would do such a thing but Ea? Ask him.'

Ea turned to Ellil and said, 'Yes, I did this thing. I saved them. For you did wrong by destroying the whole world. Why punish those who were not guilty? You could have sent lions to eat the ones who did wrong. You could have sent a famine or a plague and still achieved your goal. I did not tell this man our secret but rather sent him a vision of what was to come, and he did as he was commanded. But now you must decide his fate.'

"Ellil went into my boat. He stretched out his hand to me and to my wife and brought us aboard. He bid us kneel before him, then he touched our foreheads and said, 'You were born mortals, but from now on, you shall be immortal. Together you shall dwell in a far land, at the source of all rivers.'

"But the gods are not here. They will not gather together here for you. Perhaps if you go six days and seven nights without sleep, you will find what you seek."

Gilgamesh then sat down, to attempt what Utnapishtim said he must do, but no sooner had his body touched the ground than he was overcome with a deep sleep, and there he lay upon the ground. Utnapishtim said to his wife, "Look! He wanted to become immortal by staying awake, and the moment he touches the ground, he falls asleep!"

His wife said, "Wake him then, and send him back to his own country. Send him home, back the way he came!"

"No, I'll not do that," said Utnapishtim, "for men can be deceitful. Instead, you shall bake for him his daily bread, and each day he sleeps, place one loaf by his head. Then mark on this wall the number of days he has slumbered away. When he awakes, he will see how long he has slept."

Utnapishtim's wife did as her husband commanded her. Each day, she baked a loaf of bread and put it next to Gilgamesh's head where he slept there on the shore, and she marked the number of the days he slept on the nearby wall. One day Gilgamesh slept, then two, then three and four, then five, then six. And each loaf of bread began to harden and then molder as time went by. Finally, on the dawn of the seventh day, Utnapishtim shook Gilgamesh by the shoulder and said, "Gilgamesh, awaken!"

Gilgamesh sat up and said, "What is this? No sooner did I lay down to sleep but you awaken me!"

Utnapishtim pointed to the loaves of bread and said, "You have slept for six days and seven nights. Look here at these loaves of bread. My wife baked one for every day you slept, and you can see that they have all begun to harden and molder. Also, we marked the days of your slumber on this wall. You will see there are seven markings."

Gilgamesh sorrowed at this, saying, "Alas, for no matter where I go, Death is always there, snapping at my heels! Will I never be free of him?"

Utnapishtim then turned to Urshanabi, the boatman, and said, "Never more shall you come here. You and the man you brought are both banished from this place forever. But these tasks must you do before you bring him home. Draw a hot bath for Gilgamesh, and let him soak in it until all the dust and grime of his weary travels have been washed away. Wash his unkempt hair, and comb it out neatly. Take the beast pelts and cast them into the sea for the tide to take them where it will. And when Gilgamesh is clean and refreshed, give him clothing to wear, garments befitting his station. Restore his body to its natural beauty, so that he may go home to his people without shame."

Urshanabi did as he was commanded. He drew a bath for Gilgamesh and washed and combed his hair. He took the beast pelts and threw them into the sea. And when Gilgamesh was clean and refreshed, Urshanabi dressed him in clean garments befitting his station. Then Gilgamesh and Urshanabi boarded their boat and pushed it out into the surf.

Utnapishtim and his wife stood on the shore watching them go. Suddenly, Utnapishtim's wife said, "Wait! Call them back, for Gilgamesh leaves us without a gift befitting such a guest, a royal guest who has come here after long toil and danger."

Utnapishtim called them back, and when they had beached the boat once more, he said to Gilgamesh, "Before you go, one last secret will I impart to you. In the ocean that flows beneath the earth, there is a plant that will restore an old person's vigor, the Plant of Life. If you go down to that ocean, you will see it growing there. The plant has many thorns; have care when you pluck it! Bring it back with you, and you will have your desire."

Gilgamesh dug a great pit that opened above the ocean that flows beneath the earth. He tied great stones to his feet so that he could descend to the sea floor, then he jumped into the pit and descended to the bottom of the ocean. There he saw the thorny plant, just as Utnapishtim said. Gilgamesh grasped it, and the thorns cut his palm, but he did not pay that any mind. He cut the bonds that held the stones to his feet and rose to the surface. When he broke through into the good, clean air, he shouted, "I have found it! Now I shall be able to cheat death! But first I will test this on some old man of my city to see whether it works, and if it does, I shall take some myself!"

Urshanabi helped Gilgamesh out of the pit, and together they took ship to take Gilgamesh home to his city of Uruk. They crossed the ocean in safety, but a journey of many miles still lay before them. Together they walked in companionship, until one day they stopped by a clear pool that was surrounded by trees. The day was hot and dry, and Gilgamesh wished to refresh himself. He stripped off his clothing and lay it at the edge of the pool, along with the Plant of Life. But while Gilgamesh splashed in the water refreshing himself, a serpent passed nearby. The serpent smelled the scent of the plant and was drawn to it, so it went to the edge of the pool and carried the plant away.

When Gilgamesh came out of the pool, he saw that the plant was gone, but that the serpent had shed its skin after taking it and slithering away. Gilgamesh sat on the ground and wept. "O, all I have endured has been for naught! All the journey, and all the hardship, and all the danger, wasted! I will never again be able to find that plant, and Death shall come for me in time, as he does for everyone."

Gilgamesh and Urshanabi traveled on, stopping only to eat and sleep. And on the next day, they arrived at the city of Uruk. "There is my city, Urshanabi! Is she not glorious? Look at her strong walls, her finely crafted gates! Come, walk with me upon the walls, and you shall see how well my city is built, and how prosperous she is. You shall see the date groves and the Temple of Ishtar and many other things besides, in this, my city. Come!"

Glossary

Adad	God of weather and rain
Adapa	A wise man favored by the gods; unknowingly refuses the gift of immortality
Annunaki	The greater gods
Annunitum	A warrior goddess originally connected with **Ishtar**
Anshar	Mesopotamian god; father of **Anu**; consort of **Kishar**
Anu	Chief god of the Mesopotamian pantheon; one of the **Annunaki**
Anzu Bird	Mythical creature with the head of a lion and the body of a bird; associated with thunder
Apsu (i)	In the Babylonian creation myth, a creator god associated with sweet water
Apsu (ii)	Dwelling-place of **Enki** underground; place of underground sweet water
Aruru	Mesopotamian mother goddess; one of the **Annunaki**
Asushunamir	Eunuch created to help rescue **Ishtar** from the Underworld

Atrahasis	Survivor of the Great Flood and builder of the ark
Aw-ila	God who gives his life to create humans
Babylon	Mesopotamian city; became the seat of the Babylonian Empire and one of the most important ancient urban centers
Belet-ili	A mother goddess; mother of the hero-god **Ninurta**; one of the **Annunaki**
Belili	Sumerian deity; sister of Dumuzi (Akkadian **Tammuz**); also known as Geshtinanna
Bull of Heaven	Possibly a reference to the constellation Taurus; monstrous bull sent by **Ishtar** to kill **Gilgamesh**
Dagan	A god of fertility and agriculture
Damkina	A mother goddess; wife of **Enki**; one of the **Annunaki**
Duranki	A house of the gods
E-kur	Another name for **Duranki**
Ea	God of wisdom, creation, and mischief; often syncretic with **Enki** in Sumerian myths; one of the **Annunaki**
E-galgina	A palace within the Underworld
Ellil	God associated with winds; one of the **Annunaki**

Enki	God of wisdom, creation, and mischief; often syncretic with **Ea** in Akkadian myths; husband of **Damkina**; one of the **Annunaki**
Enkidu	A hairy, wild man sent to tame **Gilgamesh**; becomes Gilgamesh's best friend and companion in arms
Ennugi	Servant to **Ellil**; also associated with canals
Ereshkigal	Goddess of the Underworld; consort of **Nergal**
Eridu	Ancient Sumerian city; considered to be the home of **Enki**
Erra	Warrior god; also associated with the power of the sun; syncretic with **Nergal**
E-sara	House for the gods created by **Marduk**
Etana	Ancient king of **Kish**
Gilgamesh	King of Uruk and protagonist of the *Epic of Gilgamesh*
Gizzida	Sumerian Underworld deity; husband of **Belili**; also known as Ningishzida
Humbaba	A forest giant slain by **Gilgamesh** and **Enkidu**
Igigi	The lesser gods
Ilabrat	Attendant of **Anu**

Ishtar	Goddess of procreation and war; one of the **Annunaki**
Ishullanu	Man who refused to make love to **Ishtar**; mentioned in the *Epic of Gilgamesh*
Kalkal	Gatekeeper of the house of **Ellil**
Kish	Ancient Mesopotamian city-state
Kishar	Mesopotamian goddess; mother of **Anu**; consort of **Anshar**
kor	A measure of liquid volume
Lahamu	A Mesopotamian goddess; mother of **Anshar** and **Kishar**
Lahmu	A Mesopotamian god; father of **Anshar** and **Kishar**
Lugalbanda	Father of **Gilgamesh**; treated as a deity in the *Epic of Gilgamesh*
Mami	A mother goddess; one of the **Annunaki**
Marduk	Chief Babylonian creator god and hero
mina	A measure of dry weight
Mount Nimush	Mountain where the ark of **Utnapishtim** comes to rest after the Great Flood
Mountain of Mashu	Mountain under which runs the path that **Shamash** takes during the night

Mummu	Adviser to the god **Apsu**
Namtar	Adviser to **Ereshkigal**; associated with plague and disease
Nanna	God of the moon; one of the **Annunaki**
Nergal	God of war and consort of **Ereshkigal**
Nibiru	The planet Jupiter
Ninsun	Mesopotamian goddess; mother of **Gilgamesh**
Nintu	A mother goddess who helps create the human race; one of the **Annunaki**
Ninurta	A hero-god; son of **Mami**
Nusku	Adviser to **Ellil**; associated with light and fire
Papsukkal	Counsellor and servant to the **Annunaki**
Qingu	Son of **Tiamat**; rises in rebellion against the gods and is killed by **Marduk**
Shamash	God of the sun; one of the **Annunaki**
Shamhat	Prostitute who civilizes **Enkidu**
Shara	A Sumerian god of war; son of Ishtar
Shuruppak	Ancient Sumerian city on the banks of the Euphrates
Siduri	An old woman who keeps a tavern near the seashore in the Epic of Gilgamesh

Sin	God of the moon; also known as **Nanna**; one of the **Annunaki**
Tammuz	A dying-and-rising god; consort of **Ishtar**
Tiamat	Mesopotamian goddess associated with salt water; rebels against the gods and is killed by **Marduk**, who uses her body to create the world
Urshanabi	Boatman to **Utnapishtim** in the *Epic of Gilgamesh*
Uruk	Ancient Sumerian city; **Gilgamesh** is its king in the *Epic of Gilgamesh*
Utnapishtim	Man who survives the Great Flood and is granted eternal life by the gods; character in the *Epic of Gilgamesh*
Waters of Death	Band of water in the ocean that separates the land of mortal people from the place where **Utnapishtim** lives in the *Epic of Gilgamesh*

Part 2: Sumerian Mythology

Captivating Myths of Gods, Goddesses, and Legendary Creatures of Ancient Sumer and Their Importance to the Sumerians

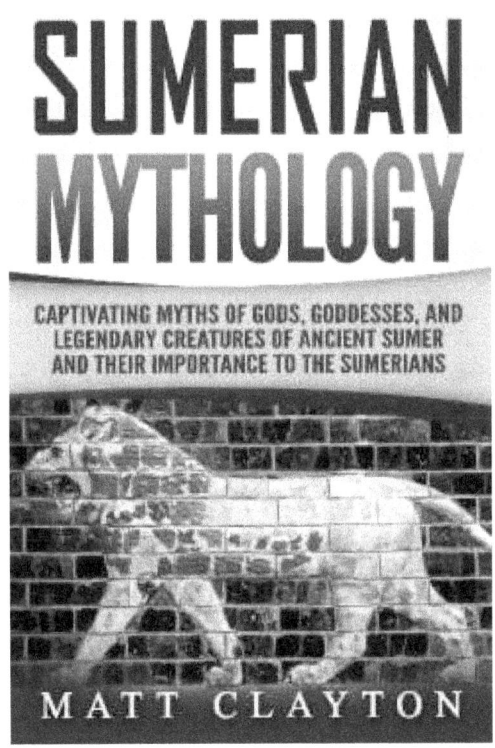

Introduction

Sumerian literature comprises one of the oldest collections of written documents in the world. Like other bodies of mythology created by myriad cultures, the Sumerian corpus contains stories explaining the origins of the world, myths of the deeds and foibles of all-too-human deities and semi-divine beings, tales of magic and miracles, and epics detailing the mighty exploits of heroes who by their great strength and skill overcome dangerous beasts and human enemies alike. Surviving texts in Sumerian also include a number of religious texts composed by Enheduanna, the daughter of Sargon of Akkad and the high priestess in the temple of the moon god Nanna, as well as the first named author in human history.

The writing system used to record Sumerian texts of all kinds is known as cuneiform, for its use of a wedge-shaped stylus to make symbols impressed into soft clay tablets that were then left to dry, or were sometimes fired in a kiln, to preserve the writing. (The word "cuneiform" has its roots in the Latin word *cuneus*, meaning "wedge.") This system, thought to be the oldest form of writing in the world, was later adapted throughout Mesopotamia by speakers of languages such as Akkadian and Old Persian. Although an untold number of these tablets have been entirely lost, thousands of them have survived into the present day. However, many of the surviving tablets have come down to us broken and therefore incomplete, leading to difficulties in translating and reconstructing the texts that first began to be written down almost five thousand years ago.

The ancient Sumerian civilization began in the so-called "Fertile Crescent," an area around and between the Tigris and Euphrates Rivers in what is now Iraq. Starting around 3000 BCE, the Sumerians occupied the southern end of this Crescent, near the mouths of the rivers and not far from the Persian Gulf. The Sumerian people were among the first in the region to practice agriculture and to create city-states. They pioneered many important techniques in metalworking, the creation of textiles, and animal husbandry, and with their invention of cuneiform writing, they not only inscribed their religious texts but also kept very meticulous records of their business dealings and created the first corpus of written law.

Sumerian is what is known as a "language isolate," meaning that it appears to have no relationship to any other languages. Sometime around 2000 BCE, Sumerian fell out of use as a spoken tongue and was replaced as a vernacular by Akkadian (a Semitic language related to modern Amharic and Arabic); however, Sumerian remained as an elite literary and ritual language for many centuries afterward. One outcome of these shifts in language use is that Sumerian texts were recorded in both monolingual Sumerian forms and also in bilingual forms alongside the Akkadian versions.

Defining what constitutes "Sumerian" myth is complicated not only by the linguistic situation but by other historical events and cultural realities. Sumer was absorbed into the Akkadian Empire in 2234 BCE, and there is a generous amount of overlap between Sumerian and Akkadian religions and mythography that can make it difficult to disentangle one from the other. Therefore, for the purposes of this book, I have followed the lists and categorization of narratives provided in the Electronic Text Corpus of Sumerian Literature (ETCSL) created by the Faculty of Oriental Studies at the University of Oxford.

The myths presented in the present volume include tales of gods and goddesses, both major and minor, as well as kings and heroes, both historical and mythical. One such king is the hero of what many scholars believe to be the first written epic: Gilgamesh. Stories about Gilgamesh—a historical Sumerian king who later became deified and mythologized—and about his illustrious (and likely mythical) forbears, Lugalbanda and Enmerkar, form an important subset of the narratives recorded in the Sumerian language, and the Sumerian myths formed the basis for the expanded Akkadian epic best known to modern readers. The tale about Sargon of Akkad is also about an actual historical figure, although one for whom we have more reliable evidence than we do for Gilgamesh. However, the events related in the story that explains how Sargon rose to kingship have been mythologized, likely as part of an attempt to provide Sargon's reign with political and religious legitimacy.

Just as the stories of Gilgamesh are set in places that are at once historical and mythical, so, too, do the tales of the gods create an overlap between the physical world and the world of myth. In Sumerian myths, Enlil lives in his house, the E-kur, in the Sumerian city of Nippur, but this is not merely a mythical house populated by mythical beings: The E-kur was the actual structure made by Sumerians as a temple for the worship of Enlil. And just as historical, physical Nippur was a place of pilgrimage in actuality, it also is in myth, as we see in the story of Nanna's journey to that city to visit his divine father, Enlil.

In addition to creating connections between the human world and the divine, Sumerian myths explain how the world came to be in the first place. These myths establish the cosmic order, which places the greater gods, or Annunaki, at the top of the hierarchy, with the lesser gods, or Igigi, below them. Below the Igigi are human beings, who, according to the Sumerians, were created to do the work of building and farming that the Igigi originally had been assigned to do, thus making human beings responsible not only for their own sustenance but for that of the gods. Other stories tell how some of the lesser deities came to be, often as the result of both rape and incest. We see this in the story of Enki and Ninhursag, for example.

Heroic strength capable of bringing mountains to their knees is the province of both male and female deities in Sumerian myth. The god Ninurta does battle with the evil Asag and rearranges the mountains to allow the Tigris and Euphrates to flow, while the goddess Inanna brings down Mount Ebih in revenge for the mountain's refusal to do the goddess reverence.

Less lofty human concerns are also encapsulated in two other myths that explain something about the interactions of differing cultures. The story of Dumuzi and Enkimdu is a mythologized version of the potential conflicts between pastoral and agricultural peoples, while the story of Martu's marriage explains the merging of the nomadic Amorite people with more settled, urbanized cultures.

The original Sumerian texts of these stories are poetic in nature and often contain a significant number of repeated phrases. For the purposes of this book, I have rendered the stories in prose and have smoothed out the repetitions in order to make the language flow as such. I have also included a glossary of names and places for modern readers who may not be familiar with Sumerian mythography. But however these stories are transmitted, they will always tell us how this ancient people understood their world and their place in it, as well as about the customs and relationships they found to be most important.

Part I: Tales of Gods and Goddesses
Enki and Ninmah

This creation myth is both unusual and important in that it deals not only with the establishment of cosmic order and how humanity came to be but also directly with the issue of human disability. Here Enki challenges Ninmah (the mother goddess also known as Ninhursag) to create a being with a flaw that cannot be fixed, but each time Ninmah presents Enki with one of her disabled creations, Enki decrees a place for them in society. After Ninmah makes several attempts to best Enki and fails, Enki declares it to be his turn to create something. When Enki creates a being that is so disabled that Ninmah cannot find a solution, the contest comes to an end, although the final portion of the story is fragmented, and it is unclear exactly what happens to Enki's creation or how Enki's apparent victory over Ninmah is decided.

In her dictionary of Near Eastern mythology, Assyriologist Gwendolyn Leick has a somewhat different interpretation for the character of Umul, the creature made by Enki. Based on the list of

Umul's characteristics, Leick suggests that rather than being a severely disabled adult, this creature is, in fact, the first baby.

When the heavens and the Earth were first created, there were only the gods and goddesses to dwell in it. The goddesses became the wives of the gods, and the gods did the work of fashioning the Earth. The Annunaki acted as planners and supervisors, determining what was to be done. The Igigi did the labor according to the Annunakis' commands. The Igigi dug the beds of the rivers, they heaped up the mountains. It was ponderous toil, and the Igigi were discontented.

While that work was going on, Enki, the god of wisdom, had retired to his chamber in the Apsu, where he took his rest. As the Annunaki planned and the Igigi toiled, Enki slept. The Igigi said amongst themselves, "It is Enki's fault that we must labor like this." But Enki slept on and did not hear their complaints.

Finally, Namma, great mother of the gods, went to Enki and woke him. "Arise from your bed, Enki. The gods are discontented with their labors and have begun to rebel. Arise from your bed, and help them. Create a substitute for them, one who can do this labor in their stead."

Enki arose from his bed and went to his council chamber, where he thought long about what should be done. Finally, he created two birth-goddesses. Then he summoned his mother Namma and said, "Take you a measure of clay and mix it with drops of my blood. When it is well mixed, cut it into portions, and with the help of your fellow goddesses, shape the pieces of clay into beings."

And so it was that Enki and the goddesses created men and women. The new beings were given life, and when the men and women saw one another, they desired to be married. Each man married one of the women, and soon they were having children of their own. Enki and the goddesses placed the new beings on the Earth and gave to them the labors that the Igigi had done before. Relieved of their tasks, the gods fell at Enki's feet and praised him for his wisdom. Then they declared a great feast to celebrate the works of Enki.

At the feast, Enki and Ninmah drank beer together. Ninmah said to Enki, "I have the power to decree the fate of human beings. I can make their bodies well or ill. This is a power I hold."

Enki answered, "Well, then, whatever fate or fashion you decree for human beings, I can change it to its opposite."

So, Ninmah took a piece of clay and fashioned it into a man with weak, withered hands that could not grasp anything. Enki looked upon him and decreed that he should be a servant to the king.

Ninmah took another piece of clay and fashioned it into a blind man. Enki gave to the blind man the gift of music and set him to sing in the presence of the king.

A third man Ninmah made, one with malformed feet. Enki gave the man with malformed feet the gift of silversmithing and set him to work making beautiful things for the king.

Then Ninmah made an incontinent man, whose urine constantly leaked from his body. Enki took the man and bathed him in water that he had blessed, and the man was cured.

Ninmah made a woman who could not bear children. Enki gave to the woman the gift of weaving and sent her to make beautiful cloth in the house of the queen.

Another person Ninmah made, one that was neither male nor female. Enki decreed that this being should be called a eunuch and that they should work as a servant in the household of the king.

Ninmah was wroth, for Enki had bested her every time. She took the last remaining piece of clay and threw it to the floor. The gods saw this, and the feasting chamber fell silent.

"You have made six beings, and I have given them gifts that they might live," said Enki. "Come now, let me create a being, and you must decree its fate."

Enki created a new being, and it was called Umul. It was weak and shriveled. All its ribs were showing. It could not hold up its head. It could neither walk nor speak. It could neither eat nor drink. Then Enki said to Ninmah, "I gave gifts to all of your creatures that they might live; now you must do the same for mine."

Ninmah went to Umul and spoke to him, but he did not answer. She offered him food, but he could not take it. She tried to help him stand, she tried to help him sit, but Umul could not do those things.

Ninmah went to Enki and said, "I do not know what to do. This being seems to be neither alive nor dead. Certainly he cannot work and will not be able to support himself."

Enki replied, "Come now. For each flawed being you created, I decreed a fate. I gave each one a gift."

[The remainder of the story is fragmented, but the surviving pieces seem to indicate that Enki won the competition. It is unclear exactly what fate was ultimately decreed for Umul, although in W. G. Lambert's translation, Enki says of Umul, "May he make my house."]

Enlil and Ninlil

Enlil was the primary god of the Sumerian pantheon. The main cult center for his worship was in the city of Nippur, where the temple dedicated to him was known as the E-kur. Enlil was the firstborn son of the great god An, and as such, he was usually thought of as a god who dispensed judgements and decreed fates. He is often associated with wind and air, and he was thought to bring both prosperity and calamity alike.

Ninlil was the consort of Enlil, and her name is actually an honorific referencing her husband's name. One version of the story of the wedding of Enlil and Ninlil states that Ninlil's name originally was Sud and that she received her new name when she married Enlil.

The primary function of the myth of Enlil and Ninlil is to explain the origins of Nanna, Nergal, Ninazu, and Enbilulu, the gods of the moon, of war and the Underworld, of boundaries, and of canals, respectively. It also positions Ninlil as a mother goddess. But as scholar Gwendolyn Leick observes in her book about the sexual and erotic aspects of Mesopotamian literature, we also can see some of the values that ancient peoples placed upon social standards for young men and women when they came of age to have children together. Leick notes that Enlil is cast out of the Ki-ur because he has had intercourse with Ninlil before marrying her.

Although we know what the E-kur was and what it was for in both its physical manifestation in ancient Nippur and in its mythical sense, the meaning of "Ki-ur" remains obscure. Assyriologist Samuel Kramer discusses the word in some footnotes to his article on the Sumerian flood myth where he suggests that it means something like "countryside," apparently referring to rural areas that, while inhabited, exist in opposition to populous cities. In the myth of Enlil and Ninlil, the "Ki-ur" appears to refer to some sort of place where the gods reside, a place that is both outside the city and that requires those who enter it to be ritually pure.

Once in the city of Nippur, there lived a young woman named Ninlil and a young man named Enlil. The young woman was very beautiful, and the young man was strong and brave. Ninlil lived with her mother, a wise old woman named Nunbarshegunu. Now, there was nothing that Ninlil liked better than to go down to the river and stroll along its banks. But Nunbarshegunu did not want her daughter to go down to the river because the young Enlil also liked to walk along the riverbanks and sail on the water.

"Stay away from the river," said Nunbarshegunu, "and you must never bathe in it! That young Enlil is always there. What if he sees you walking along the holy river or bathing in it? What if he sees you and desires you, and what if he has his way with you? What will you do then?"

Ninlil did not listen to her mother. Every day, she went down to the river and walked along its banks. One day, Enlil happened to be at the river at the same time as Ninlil. Enlil saw how beautiful Ninlil was, and he was entranced. Enlil went up to Ninlil and said, "You are so beautiful! Please let me kiss you, let me lie with you! Do not turn me away, for I love you!"

But Ninlil would not let Enlil lie with her. She said, "I am too young to kiss any man and certainly too young to lie with him. What if you get me with child? What will I do then? Besides, if my mother and father found out what we had done, they would be wroth with me."

And so, Ninlil went away, and Enlil did not get his desire.

Enlil did not know what to do next, so he went to speak to Nuska, the Master Builder of the E-kur, the House of the Gods. "Nuska," said Enlil, "do you know that young woman who walks along the river every day? Her name is Ninlil, and she is very beautiful. Tell me, does she have any other suitors? Has anyone ever kissed her before?"

For answer, Nuska said, "Get into my boat, O Enlil, and I will take you to her." Nuska sailed them down the river, and all along the way, Enlil thought to himself how delightful it would be to finally kiss Ninlil and to finally lie together.

Soon enough, Enlil found Ninlil. He kissed her and poured his seed into her womb, and Ninlil was got with child. And thus it was that Ninlil bore Nanna, the god of the moon.

Then Enlil went to the Ki-ur for he had a mind to wander about there. But the gods had seen what he had done with Ninlil, and they had him arrested. The gods told Enlil that for his deed he was to be cast out of the city for he was now impure.

Enlil went to the gates to leave the city. Ninlil saw him go and followed behind him. Enlil knew that Ninlil was there and did not want Ninlil to follow him. He did not want her to know where he was going. When Enlil arrived at the city gates, he went to the gatekeeper and said, "Do you see the beautiful Ninlil who follows me? If she asks where I have gone, you must tell her that you do not know."

Ninlil arrived at the gate. She asked the gatekeeper where Enlil had gone. But the gatekeeper was not there; Enlil had taken his form and taken his place. In the form of the gatekeeper, Enlil said, "I have not seen him at all, my lady. I do not know where he is."

"Well," said Ninlil, "if that is the case, then you must come and lie with me once I have had my child. For this is Enlil's child, and since he is your lord, that makes me your lady."

The gatekeeper and Ninlil lay together and delighted in one another. Enlil poured his seed into her womb, and Ninlil was got with child. And thus it was that Ninlil bore Nergal, the god of war and the Underworld.

Then Enlil went to the Id-kura, the river that flows between the land of the living and the Underworld, and Ninlil followed him. Enlil went to the man who dwelt beside the Id-kura and said, "Do you see the beautiful Ninlil who follows me? If she asks where I have gone, you must tell her that you do not know."

Ninlil arrived at the river. She asked the man who dwelt beside the river where Enlil had gone. But the man was not there; Enlil had taken his form and taken his place. In the form of the man who dwelt by the Id-kura, Enlil said, "I have not seen him at all, my lady. I do not know where he is."

"Well," said Ninlil, "if that is the case, then you must come and lie with me once I have had my child. For this is Enlil's child, and since he is your lord, that makes me your lady."

The man who dwelt by the Id-kura and Ninlil lay together and delighted in one another. Enlil poured his seed into her womb, and Ninlil became heavy with child. And thus it was that Ninlil bore Ninazu, the god who sets the boundaries of the fields.

Then Enlil left Ninlil and went walking along the river, and Ninlil followed him. Enlil went to the ferryman and said, "Do you see the beautiful Ninlil who follows me? If she asks where I have gone, you must tell her that you do not know."

Ninlil arrived at the river. She asked the ferryman where Enlil had gone. But the man was not there; Enlil had taken his form and taken his place. In the form of the ferryman, Enlil said, "I have not seen him at all, my lady. I do not know where he is."

"Well," said Ninlil, "if that is the case, then you must come and lie with me once I have had my child. For this is Enlil's child, and since he is your lord, that makes me your lady."

The ferryman and Ninlil lay together and delighted in one another. Enlil poured the seed of Enbilulu into her womb, and Ninlil was got with child. And thus it was that Ninlil bore Enbilulu, the god of canals.

Enki and Ninhursag

This story is set in the land of Dilmun, a place that is synonymous with peace and plenty in Sumerian literature. An actual historical Dilmun did exist; scholars have located it on the eastern side of the Arabian Peninsula along the Persian Gulf. Dilmun likely included what is now the island nation of Bahrain and the peninsula that is now the state of Qatar, and it was an important trading partner for Mesopotamian peoples. Over time, however, Dilmun became mythologized in Sumerian literature as a kind of paradise where there was neither sickness nor violence.

Enki, one of the main characters in this myth, is a creator god, a trickster, and is particularly associated with water. Enki also seems to have been conceived of as a sort of opposite to Enlil. In her dictionary of Near Eastern myth, Assyriologist Gwendolyn Leick notes that the name Enlil may be translated as "Lord Air," while Enki can be rendered as "Lord Earth." Whereas Enlil's primary cult center was in Nippur, Enki's main temple was in Eridu, a city in what is now south-central Iraq, to the west of the Euphrates River.

"Ninhursag" is but one of the many names of the Sumerian great mother goddess. Ninhursag is particularly associated with Enki, and according to Leick, the goddess' name is actually a title meaning

something like "Lady of the Wild Hills," a name that is given to her by her heroic son, Ninurta, in the myth of his battle against the evil Asag creature.

This story explains the origins of several lesser deities. First are Ninsar, Ninkura, and Uttu, who were associated with plants, mountain pastures, and weaving, respectively. As is common in ancient mythology, divine beings in Sumerian tales are often the products of incestuous relations, and this story participates in that tradition. Enki first has relations with Ninhursag and then with Ninsar, the daughter who is produced by that union, and then with her daughter Ninkura, and so on, until the fourth generation is reached with Uttu, whereupon Ninhursag puts a stop to the pattern by removing Enki's seed from her great-granddaughter's womb and uses it to create plants instead. When Enki consumes the plants without asking, Ninhursag departs in a rage and does not come back until a fox is sent by the Annunaki to fetch her. The story ends with Ninhursag healing Enki from the illness caused by her absence, and several more minor deities are named and possibly created in the process.

The original tablets containing this story are broken in places, as is common with these very ancient and very fragile documents. In some places it is possible to imagine what might have transpired in the parts of the story that are missing based on context, when there is enough material to make a guess at what happened. However, the portion of the story that shows how the fox brought Ninhursag back to the Annunaki is too scantily preserved to be recreated with any accuracy. I have noted this in the text of the myth at the appropriate point. Likewise, in the section where Ninhursag heals an ailing Enki piece by piece, some of the words for the affected body parts are missing or untranslatable and cannot be guessed from context. I have therefore replaced these with ellipses.

Far, far away, there is a land called Dilmun. Dilmun is a pure land, a land of peace and of plenty. Beasts of prey hunt not, carrion birds feed not. In Dilmun there is no sickness and no fear, there is no slow decline into agedness, and there is no death and no mourning. Toil and travail are known not. All is young, all is peaceful, all is pure, and there in that land of Dilmun did Enki lie with his consort in great joy.

One day, Ninsikila went to her father Enki and said, "O my father, all is well in Dilmun, all is peaceful and pure, but our city has no water. We have no river upon which to build a quay or sail boats. We have no canals to water our fields. There are no ponds that the beasts may drink from. Our wells are dry, and the people have nothing to drink. Give to us water, that we might live."

Enki thought upon Ninsikila's request and said, "When Utu the sun god appears in the sky, then shall Dilmun have water."

And so it was that when Utu the sun god rose in the sky, water began to flow in Dilmun. A great river wound its way through the city, a river on which to build a quay, on which to sail boats, and Dilmun was able to trade with other peoples. Water flowed through the canals, watering the fields, and the crops grew in abundance. Ponds filled with good, sweet water, and the beasts drank their fill. Wells filled with good, sweet water, and the people drank their fill.

Then Enki invited the goddess Ninhursag to lie with him. "Come," he said, "let us delight in one another."

Ninhursag lay with Enki, and he poured his seed into her, and she was got with child. For nine days did Ninhursag carry that child, and each day was like a month. After nine days, the child was born, a girl named Ninsar.

One day, Enki went down to the riverbank, and there he saw Ninsar, who was walking along the river on the other side, Ninsar who had grown into a beautiful, young woman. Enki went to his counselor, Isimud, and said, "Is Ninsar not of an age to be kissed? Is she not ready to know a man?"

Isimud answered, "Yes, indeed, she is of an age. Come, get into my boat, and I will sail you over to her."

Enki crossed the river in Isimud's boat. He went to Ninsar and kissed her. Enki took Ninsar and laid her on the ground and poured his seed into her. He poured his seed into her, and she was got with child. For nine days did Ninsar carry that child, and each day was like a month. After nine days, the child was born, a girl named Ninkura.

On another day, Enki went down to the riverbank, and there he saw Ninkura, who was walking along the river on the other side, Ninkura who had grown into a beautiful, young woman. Enki went to his counselor, Isimud, and said, "Is Ninkura not of an age to be kissed? Is she not ready to know a man?"

Isimud answered, "Yes, indeed, she is of an age. Come, get into my boat, and I will sail you over to her."

Enki crossed the river in Isimud's boat. He went to Ninkura and kissed her. Enki took Ninkura and lay her on the ground and poured his seed into her. He poured his seed into her, and she was got with child. For nine days did Ninkura carry that child, and each day was like a month. After nine days, the child was born, a girl named Uttu.

When Uttu came of age, her great-grandmother Ninhursag took her aside and said, "Uttu, you are now of an age where men may begin to look upon you and desire you. You must be very careful when you walk down at the river's edge. Be careful, because Enki often stands on the opposite bank and watches the young women as they go by. If Enki approaches you, do not give him what he wants right away. Tell him that he must first bring to you cucumbers and grapes and apples, all ripe and sweet and juicy, and that when he does so, he will have what he desires."

And so it was that one day Uttu went walking along the riverbank, and she was very beautiful to behold. On the other side of the river, Enki watched Uttu, and he desired her. Once again, Enki's counselor sailed him to the other side of the river, and Enki made known his desire to Uttu.

Uttu remembered Ninhursag's instruction and said, "You will have what you desire only when you bring me cucumbers and grapes and apples, all ripe and sweet and juicy."

"How shall I do that," said Enki, "when all the fields are dry and dusty, and the gardener weeps under his withering trees?"

"I do not know how you are to do those things, only that you will not have what you desire without them."

Enki went to the garden, where all was dry and dusty. He made water flow into the canals. He made water flow into the channels. He made water flow into the furrows. Soon, the garden was bearing all manner of good things, and the gardener danced in his joy. The gardener gave cucumbers, grapes, and apples to Enki, all ripe and sweet and juicy. The gardener heaped cucumbers, grapes, and apples into the lap of Enki, as thanks for the water that made his garden flourish.

Enki took the cucumbers, grapes, and apples to the house of Uttu. He knocked upon her door. From within, Uttu said, "Who is there?"

"It is I, the gardener, bearing cucumbers and grapes and apples," said Enki.

Uttu let him in with great joy. Enki gave to her the cucumbers, grapes, and apples, all ripe and sweet and juicy. And in Uttu's house, they lay together and delighted in one another. Enki poured his seed into Uttu's womb, but Uttu lamented having lain with him. Ninhursag then took the seed from Uttu and planted it in her garden. From Enki's seed grew eight plants with their fruit, and Ninhursag tended them.

One day, Enki said to his counselor Isimud, "Tell me, what of the plants that grew from my seed that Ninhursag planted? Are they grown? Have they fruited? Go to Ninhursag's garden, and see what is growing there."

And so, Isimud went to Ninhursag's garden. He looked over the wall and saw the eight plants growing there, the eight tall plants with their fruit. He saw that the fruit was good to eat and thought that his master might wish to taste of it. So, Isimud cut down the eight plants. He cut them down with their fruit and brought them back to Enki. Enki tasted of their fruit, and it was very good.

When Ninhursag found out that Isimud had cut down the plants and taken them to Enki that he might eat of them, she flew into a rage and cursed Enki. "Never again shall I look upon you!" she said, and then she went away and did not come back.

The Annunaki waited and waited for Ninhursag to return. When she did not, the Annunaki became despondent. They sat in the dust and mourned the loss of Ninhursag.

A fox trotted past and saw the Annunaki and their sorrow. The fox said, "Why is it that you sit in the dust in mourning?"

The Annunaki answered, "We mourn because Ninhursag has left us, and she does not return."

"What will you give me if I return her to you?" said the fox.

Enlil replied, "If you bring back Ninhursag, I will plant a garden for you. I will plant an orchard for you, and your name will always be remembered of the people and the gods."

[The next portion of the story is missing from the tablets. From what little remains, we can gather that the fox disguises himself in some way and is able to get Ninhursag to return to the Annunaki, where she finds them still sitting in the dust in mourning.]

Ninhursag went to Enki where he sat despondent in the dust. Ninhursag said to him, "O my brother, what is it that hurts you?"

Enki said, "My ... it is that hurts me."

Ninhursag said, "I gave birth to the god Abu for you that you might be healed. What else is it that hurts you?"

"My jaw it is that hurts me."

Ninhursag said, "I gave birth to the god Nintul for you that you might be healed. What else is it that hurts you?"

"My tooth it is that hurts me."

Ninhursag said, "I gave birth to the goddess Ninsutu for you that you might be healed. What else is it that hurts you?"

"My mouth it is that hurts me."

Ninhursag said, "I gave birth to the goddess Ninkasi for you that you might be healed. What else is it that hurts you?"

"My ... hurts me."

Ninhursag said, "I gave birth to the goddess Nazi for you that you might be healed. What else is it that hurts you?"

"My arm it is that hurts me."

Ninhursag said, "I gave birth to the goddess Azimua for you that you might be healed. What else is it that hurts you?"

"My side it is that hurts me."

Ninhursag said, "I gave birth to the goddess Ninti for you that you might be healed. What else is it that hurts you?"

"My ... hurts me."

Ninhursag said, "I gave birth to the god Enshagag for you that you might be healed."

Then Ninhursag said, "And now let us say what is to become of these gods and goddesses I have birthed. Abu shall be lord of the plants. Nintul shall be the lord of Magan. Ninsutu shall marry Ninazu, son of Enlil and Ninlil. Ninkasi shall satisfy all desires. Nazi shall marry the god Nindara. Azimua shall marry Ningishzida, son of Ninazu. Ninti shall be queen of the months, and Enshagag shall rule over Dilmun as lord."

The Exploits of Ninurta

The hero-god who slays the monstrous beast is a commonplace figure in world mythology. In the ancient Middle East, this role was played by the god Ninurta. Ninurta is the son of Enlil and Ninhursag and was originally associated with agriculture and fertility. He also is posited as a judge who rules upon points of law.

In this story, Ninurta must fight the Asag, a type of demon or dragon who is going about the land fomenting rebellion against the gods. The Asag recruits stone warriors to help him, and none but Ninurta has the strength to defeat the Asag and his army.

Besides being a tale of heroic deeds and dragon-slaying, this story also explains the origins of irrigation and agriculture as practices initiated by Ninurta in the wake of the Asag's death and assigns the title "Ninhursag," which means something like "Lady of the Wild Hills," to the goddess Ninmah. The myth of Ninurta's exploits also explains the uses and qualities of several different types of stone. While the names of some of the stones have been translated, the identification of most others remains obscure. The section of the myth in which Ninurta declares the fates of the stones is lengthy and somewhat abstruse; here it has been telescoped for a modern audience.

The hero Ninurta sat among the Annunaki at the feast that was called to honor him. Everyone was rejoicing, especially Ninurta, who drank and drank. Even more than An, even more than Enlil did Ninurta drink. And while they were feasting, Bau, goddess of healing, brought before him petitions and Ninurta, son of Enlil, gave his rulings upon them.

As Ninurta decided and the Annunaki feasted, the Sharur, the mighty battle-mace of Ninurta, suddenly cried out, saying, "O my master, O Lord Ninurta, O Ninurta, hero who is the mightiest of all and whom none may withstand, I tell you that the Asag has come forth and is wreaking havoc upon the land. The Asag is a warrior, a fell creature who has no father and who grew and was nourished despite never suckling at the breast. He is arrogant and ambitious, and he comes forth to challenge all.

"The Asag lives in the mountains, and its offspring are many. Even the plants count him king among them. He has called the stones to him. He has called emery and diorite, flint and alabaster, and many more besides, and made an army of them, and with that army, he raids cities far and near. Even the gods of those cities bow before his might, and now, the Asag sits in majesty and metes out justice, usurping the place of the gods. The people live in terror of the Asag, and even the mountains make offerings to him.

"Listen to my words, O mighty one! Listen to what I have to say, for I bring you the pleas of the people. They ask you to come to them and to rid them of the Asag, for none may stand against it but you, O son of Enlil! Be swift in your decision, for day by day your power among the people wanes. They say that if you will not help them, then you will no longer be king over them, and the Asag in his arrogance believes that he can take your place. Day by day he moves into new places and conquers them. Soon, all the Earth will be in his thrall if you do not act!

"But you are the raging bull, you are the swift antelope, and surely you will conquer the Asag. You will conquer the Asag even though his armies are too numerous to be counted, even though no hero has yet been able to defeat the Asag, even though no weapon has yet been able to wound the Asag. What say you, O mighty one? What say you to the insolence of the Asag, to his conquest of cities that rightfully belong to the gods?"

Ninurta heard the words of the Sharur, and he rose out of his seat, crying, "Alas!" He cried with such a great voice that the Earth shook and the heavens trembled. Enlil and the other gods also were shaken and left the E-kur. Mountains fell down before Ninurta's cry, and the Earth was darkened. Ninurta raged in his anger against the Asag, and the Annunaki fled before his anger. Then Ninurta took up his mace and his lance and readied himself for battle. Evil winds he summoned to his aid, winds that brought down a rain of hot coals that consumed all they touched, winds that toppled every tree in their path, winds that made waves upon the Tigris and stirred up her sediments so that her waters were muddied.

Ninurta went to the quay to take a ship on his way to meet the Asag. At the riverside, all the people quailed at the rage of Ninurta. They ran away, blinded by their fear. The birds tried to flee, but the winds of Ninurta made their wings useless. The fish tried to flee, but the storms of Ninurta flung them up onto the shore, where they lay gasping and drowning in air. The cattle and sheep tried to flee, but the fire of Ninurta's anger roasted them where they stood. Even the mountains could not withstand Ninurta's rage, for the floodwaters rose up their banks and washed away everything in their path.

Striding into the lands held by the Asag, Ninurta laid waste their cities; he made captives of their people. He slew the messengers of the Asag; he caused a flood of poison to run through the land, killing all it touched. The rage of Ninurta engulfed the land, and none could withstand his onslaught.

Rejoicing in battle, Ninurta turned to the Sharur and smiled upon it. The Sharur flew away by itself, bringing down mountains for Ninurta, taking prisoners for him, and flying high above the Earth to see what might be seen. Those who saw it flying would give it news to take back to its master, news about the Asag and his armies. When all the news had been gathered, the Sharur returned to Ninurta and said, "Lo! O mighty Ninurta, whose strength none might resist, you have conquered the rebellious places, and already you have slain many of the Asag's warriors. But do not go yet into the mountains to meet the Asag! Verily you are well made and well born, verily you are most beautiful, verily you are greatest in strength and all tremble before you, but do not meet the Asag yet! Do not take your army into the mountains! The time is not yet ripe, and you will not be victorious!"

Ninurta heard the wise words of the Sharur, but he did not heed them. Instead, he marshalled his armies and marched them into the mountains. The Asag saw the approach of Ninurta and armed himself for battle. He pulled down the sky itself and fashioned it into a club. The Asag slithered along the ground like a serpent, ravening like a mad dog. The Asag fell upon Ninurta, howling its rage with a voice that was heard in every corner of the Earth, and none could withstand the passage of that fell beast throughout the land. The waters dried up in their courses, and the trees toppled onto the ground. The reeds were set aflame at the riverside, and the Asag's body carved great furrows into the ground, leaving the Earth gaping with wounds. All the people fled before the Asag as the sky turned red as blood and the crops rotted in the fields. An himself was overwhelmed, Enlil himself fled and hid from the approach of the Asag, and all the Annunaki trembled and sighed with fear.

Enlil cried out, "Who is there to protect us now that Ninurta has gone away to war? Who will keep us safe while the great hero is gone away?"

[The next section is fragmentary, but apparently, the Sharur goes to speak with Enlil about the Asag. Enlil makes a statement encouraging Ninurta to battle fiercely, and the Sharur returns to Ninurta with its report.]

The Sharur returned to its master and said, "O my master, Enlil has spoken, and this is what he says: 'Go forth, O mighty Flood! Go forth and take the Asag. Grip him by the shoulder, impale him on your spear. Take him captive, and drag him here to the E-kur. Do this, and you will never want for praise from all the peoples.'

"Go forth, O my master!" said the Sharur. "Go forth and assail the Asag, for he has built himself a rampart. He has built himself a fortress that cannot be breached, and his lust for destruction never abates."

Ninurta took heart from the words of the Sharur and of Enlil. Ninurta let forth his battle cry, and the day darkened as though it were night.

The Sharur flew into the heavens, raising a great wind that scattered the people like dry leaves. The great mace went to the mountains and set them ablaze. It went through the ranks of the enemy and crushed their skulls. Ninurta's mighty lance flew through the air, and wherever it landed, it opened a crack in the earth. The cracks filled with blood, and the stray dogs licked it up. Ninurta's weapons wrought great destruction throughout the land, and the Asag saw it but was not dismayed.

The Sharur returned to Ninurta and said, "All we do is to no avail! My lord, do not bring battle to the Asag, for he is the foul stench of a festering wound and the pus that flows from it. No matter what you command him to do, he will not obey. Wherever he goes, the land is laid waste and barren, and no one can capture him or withstand his approach. The Asag has dried up all the waters and blows through the lands like a whirlwind. The people cower in their homes, for none may stand against the Asag."

But Ninurta would not stand aside. He faced the mountains and let out a full-throated battle cry, a cry of an entire army calling for death. Ninurta strode about the country, dealing death to all his enemies. The great hero raged about, and from his mountain perch, the Asag saw the fury of the hero Ninurta. Soon enough, Ninurta rampaged his way up the Asag's mountain, and the Asag quailed at the fury of the great hero's approach. The Asag was scattered like drops of water; he was uprooted like weeds from a field. Ninurta flew at the Asag, and in his fury, he crushed the Asag like a grindstone crushes grain in a mill. And not until the foul creature lay dead at Ninurta's feet did the rage of Ninurta begin to subside.

The sun finally set at the end of that terrible day. Ninurta went to the river and washed his weapons in the flowing water. He washed the blood from his clothing and armor, and he washed the blood from his own body. And when all had been cleansed, he stood astride the body of the Asag and sang a victory song.

In the calm that followed the battle, the Annunaki came to where Ninurta stood over the body of the Asag. The gods saw the broken body of that huge monster and marveled at the strength of Ninurta. They prostrated themselves at the feet of the hero and gave him praise for his deeds. The Sharur also praised Ninurta, saying, "None can compare to you, O Ninurta! None can match your strength or your valor! Behold how the gods prostrate themselves at your feet!"

Ninurta addressed the assembled gods. "From this day henceforth, the name of this creature shall not be Asag. Instead, we shall call it Stone, and its entrails shall become the Underworld."

Then Ninurta rested from his labors. He set aside his club, and he rested from his battles.

It was at that time that the land began to dry up. The streams and wells went dry. The Tigris itself shriveled up, and its waters did not reach the sea. Workers went out with shovels and hoes, they went out to dig canals to bring water to the fields, but there was no water to be had. The crops withered in the fields, and the farmers had nothing to bring to market. Famine settled upon the land. No one had the strength to till the fields, and the grain sat scattered upon the soil.

Ninurta looked upon the people in their drought and famine and took pity upon them. He went into the mountains and made a great pile of stones and put into it a sluice gate. He gathered together the waters of the mountains and then let them flow through the sluice into the Tigris. The waters flooded into the riverbed and then up over the banks and into the fields. Soon everywhere there was enough water, and the barley grew heavy with grain in the fields, and the trees in the orchards grew heavy with fruit. The people rejoiced in this. They traded their harvest with peoples of other nations, and they gave great thanks to Ninurta and his father.

Now, at this time, the goddess Ninmah looked upon what her son Ninurta had wrought in the mountains, and she sorrowed because the mountains were no longer a place where she could go. So, Ninmah made a song of lament and went to Ninurta and sang it. Ninmah sang, "I sing 'alas' for the mountains, for they have bowed before the might of Ninurta. I sing 'alas' for the mountains, for they could not withstand his strength, the strength of the mighty hero I bore for the god Enlil. The son of Enlil will not turn his gaze to me, but I shall go to him and gaze upon him. I shall go to him with my lament, and he will see my tears."

Ninurta hearkened to the lament of Ninmah, and he said to her, "Lady Ninmah, well do I remember that when I went into the dangers of battle, you were always there with me. Behold, I have made a pile of stones here, and let this become a new mountain, and you shall be Ninhursag, which is 'Lady of the Mountain.' And I decree that your mountain shall become fecund and a place of great joy. It will bring forth herbs and grasses and fragrant cedars. It will bring forth fruit trees heavy with fruit. In its heart will be gold and silver and all manner of gems. On its sides, the wild beasts and birds will multiply. And you shall have no rival there on that mountain, not even the god An shall approach your queenly splendor. This is my gift to you, O great lady. Rejoice, and be exalted!"

When Ninurta had finished decreeing the fate of the mountains, the lady Aruru, the eldest sister of Enlil, came to him and said, "My lord, you are the greatest hero of them all. You have decreed the fate of the mountains, but what of the fate of those you slew in your battle with the Asag?"

And so, Ninurta addressed the fate of the stone warriors who had sided with the Asag. To the emery stone, flint, and others who had turned against him, Ninurta pronounced punishments. To the alabaster, diorite, hematite, and other stones who had fought on Ninurta's side, he gave great honors.

When all the fates of the stones had been assigned, Ninurta made his way out of the mountains and across the desert. Whenever he came across a village or a city, the people gathered to rejoice over him and sing his praises. On and on he strode, until he came to the river where his own barge was moored, and there the boatmen bowed down before him and sang a song praising him for his deeds. "Who is like Ninurta? Who has his strength or his skill? No enemy can stand against him! Praise to the son of Enlil!"

Then Enlil looked upon Ninurta and gave him a blessing. "O Ninurta, great is your courage and your strength! It was wise to send you to meet the Asag, for none other could have defeated him. All of your enemy's cities have been reduced to ruins, and their rulers made captive. As your reward, you shall receive a heavenly mace and power to rule over all, and eternal life besides."

And so it was that Ninurta killed the Asag, gathered up a pile of stones, and brought the waters down into the fields to make them bear grain and fruit in their seasons. So well had Ninurta healed the land that great mounds of grain were harvested and placed into the granaries. Ninurta gave the grain and the granaries into the care of the lady Nisaba, she who makes green things grow upon the Earth.

The Journey of Nanna to Nippur

One subgenre of Sumerian myth is that of a god's journey to the Sumerian city of Nippur, the primary cult center of the god Enlil, who stood at the head of the Sumerian pantheon. Such journey myths are extant for the gods Enki and Ninurta, in addition to the myth about Nanna presented here. In this story, the moon god Nanna (also known as Nanna-Suen, Suen, or Sin) determines that he should leave his home city of Ur, where his own primary cult center was located, to go to Nippur to visit his mother, the goddess Ninlil, and his father, the god Enlil. Nanna therefore causes a barge to be constructed and lades it with all manner of goods to take home as gifts.

The barge's progress along the river from Ur to Nippur has a ritual aspect in that at every city along the way, the local goddess comes out to greet Nanna and make offerings and grant well wishes, but the barge tells each one that it cannot stop for it is bound for Nippur. Assyriologist Jeremy Black notes that the list of bypassed cities likely reflects actual places one might have expected to encounter along a river journey between Ur and Nippur in ancient times. Further, Black notes that the myth of Nanna's journey reinforces Nanna's function as a god of both fertility and agriculture, especially in his causing an increase in his flocks and herds so that he can give the young produced by his animals as gifts.

There came a time when the god Nanna decided to make a journey to Nippur. Nippur was the city of his father, Enlil, and of his mother, Ninlil. "I shall journey to Nippur," Nanna said, "for I have a mind to visit my mother and my father. I have a mind to visit the lovely city of Nippur and its beautiful sanctuary. I have a mind to visit the strong city of Nippur where the palm trees grow, where palm trees grew even before Dilmun existed. I have a mind to visit the city of my mother who dresses always in the finest linen garments."

It was a long river journey from Nanna's city of Ur to Nippur, and so, Nanna would need a barge, for he wished to take many good gifts to his mother and father. Nanna sent far and wide for the materials to make his barge. Reeds came from Tummal, and pitch from the Apsu. Cypress and cedar, pine and juniper came from the forests and the mountains. When all the needed things were assembled, the workmen began to build the barge.

While the barge was being constructed, Nanna assembled all the gifts he wanted to bring to his parents. Nanna chose fine bulls and sheep from his flocks. He gathered up turtles and birds and fish. Nanna filled many baskets with fresh eggs to take to Enlil's house in Nippur.

Nanna turned loose the rams among his flock of sheep, and six hundred of his ewes dropped fine lambs as gifts for Enlil. Nanna turned male goats loose among his herd of goats, and six hundred female goats dropped fine kids as gifts for Enlil. Nanna did the same with his herds of cattle, letting the bulls loose among the cows, and six hundred cows gave birth to fine calves to be taken as gifts for Enlil.

When the barge was made well and sturdily, and when it was all laden with the gifts of Nanna to Enlil and Ninlil, it set sail along the river. The barge departed Ur and sailed along the river toward Enegir. As the barge approached Enegir, the goddess Ningirida came out of her house and set out an offering of flour. She brought with her a great vat of oil, and she cried out, "Let me anoint you with this fine oil! May you ever have wine and all good things in abundance!"

But the barge did not stop at Enegir. It sailed past, crying out, "I cannot stop! I am bound for Nippur!"

The barge departed Enegir and sailed along the river to Larsa. As the barge approached Larsa, the goddess Sherida came out of her house and set out an offering of flour. She brought with her a great vat of oil, and she cried out, "Let me anoint you with this fine oil! May you ever have wine and all good things in abundance!"

But the barge did not stop at Larsa. It sailed past, crying, "I cannot stop! I am bound for Nippur!"

The barge departed Larsa and sailed along the river to Uruk. As the barge approached Uruk, the goddess Inanna came out of her house and set out an offering of flour. She brought with her a great vat of oil, and she cried out, "Let me anoint you with this fine oil! May you ever have wine and all good things in abundance!"

But the barge did not stop at Uruk. It sailed past, crying, "I cannot stop! I am bound for Nippur!"

The barge departed Uruk and sailed along the river to Shuruppag. As the barge approached Shuruppag, the goddess Ninunuga came out of her house and set out an offering of flour and bran. She brought with her a great vat of oil, and she cried out, "Let me anoint you with this fine oil! May you ever have wine and all good things in abundance!"

But the barge did not stop at Shuruppag. It sailed past, crying, "I cannot stop! I am bound for Nippur!"

The barge departed Shuruppag and sailed along the river to Tummal. As the barge approached Tummal, the goddess Ninlil came out of her house and set out an offering of flour and bran. She brought with her a great vat of oil, and she cried out, "Let me anoint you with this fine oil! May you ever have wine and all good things in abundance!"

But the barge did not stop at Tummal. It sailed past, crying, "I cannot stop! I am bound for Nippur!"

At last, the barge departed Tummal and sailed to Nippur. Nanna sailed the barge to the quay that belonged to Enlil, and there he docked. Nanna called out to the porter who kept the gates of Enlil, "O Kalkal! O porter of my father's house! Open the door to me! Open the gates of my father's house!

"Behold, I, Nanna, have come with a barge laden with many gifts. I have bulls and sheep and goats. I have turtles and small birds. I have fish and I have eggs. Open the door to me!

"I, Nanna, on my journey did bring the lambs that were dropped by the ewes of my flock and the kids that were dropped by the goats of my flock and the calves that were dropped by the cows of my herd. All of these I gave as gifts as I sailed along the Surungal Canal, and my barge is heavy yet with gifts to be given to Enlil and Ninlil. Open the door, Kalkal! Open the door of my father's house!"

Kalkal heard the cry of Nanna, son of Enlil, and in great joy, he opened the gates to him. And there, in the house of Enlil, did Nanna give his gifts to his mighty father, and joyously did Enlil receive them.

"Welcome, my son!" cried Enlil. "Welcome again to my house! Let us eat together! Let us eat of sweet cakes together and of bread and beer!" Enlil called to his servants and commanded them to bring cakes for Nanna to eat. He commanded his servants to gather bread and beer from the E-kur to be given to Nanna to eat.

Nanna ate all the good food Enlil put before him and drank all the good drink, and he said, "O my father, O mighty Enlil, truly I am content with this good food and this good drink. Truly you are the god who gives all in abundance!

"Now it is time for me to return home to Ur, but first I ask you to fill my rivers with good fish. I ask you to fill my fields with barley heavy in the ear. Give me reeds along the rivers and wild sheep in the hills. Give me good trees in the forest and fruit for syrup and wine in the orchards. And give to me a long life, for it is time for me to return home to Ur!"

Everything Nanna asked for, Enlil gave him. He filled the rivers with good fish and the fields with barley heavy in the ear. Enlil gave Nanna reeds along the rivers and wild sheep in the hills. Enlil gave Nanna good trees in the forest and fruit for syrup and wine in the orchards, and to Nanna himself, he gave a long life.

Praise be to Enlil where he sits on his throne, and to Ninlil, mother of Nanna!

Inanna and Ebih

Male deities such as Ninurta are not the only ones who go forth to do battle with monstrous creatures in the mountains. In this story, the goddess Inanna girds herself for war to get revenge on Ebih, a mountain that refuses to bow down before her in worship. We see here the more violent of the two sides of Inanna, who in addition to being the goddess of love and procreation was the goddess of war, which is often referred to as "the game of Inanna" in Sumerian texts.

Inanna was one of the more powerful goddesses of the Sumerian pantheon, bearing the title "Queen of Heaven." She later became identified with the Akkadian/Babylonian goddess Ishtar. One myth that explains the origin of Inanna's might says that she stole some of Enki's me, *a Sumerian word denoting power or authority, after Enki had too much to drink at a banquet. Inanna sails with the* me *back to her city of Uruk, fending off the attempts of Enki and his demons to retrieve the stolen powers.*

The myth of Inanna and Ebih retold below, which shows Inanna wielding her powers of vengeance and destruction, names several places that Inanna visits in her wanderings, specifically Elam, Subir, and the Lulubi Mountains. Elam was a region on the northeastern shore of the Persian Gulf, in what is now Iran, while Subir was far to the north of Sumer, in Upper Mesopotamia. The Lulubi Mountains are an area within the Zagros range, in a portion that now lies on the border between Iraq and Iran. In her retelling of this myth, author Betty De Shong Meador notes that Mount Ebih "has been identified as the modern Jebel Hamrin," a mountain ridge that runs along the western side of the Zagros Mountains.

This myth also has special importance as part of the first piece of written literature for which we have the author's name, since it forms part of a longer work called "The Exaltation of Inanna" by a woman named Enheduanna. Enheduanna was the daughter of Sargon of Akkad, founder of the Akkadian Empire, and was high priestess of both Inanna and Nanna in the Sumerian city of Ur in the 23rd century BCE. "The Exaltation of Inanna" functions both as praise of the goddess and as a semi-autobiographical work, since it references Enheduanna's expulsion from Ur by her brother, Rimush, and her reinstatement in the temple there.

Great was the goddess Inanna, daughter of Nanna the god of the moon, and great her power. Fearsome in battle was she, clad in armor, laying waste to armies with her weapons and the strength of her arm. For her strength was that of the wild bull, and her fierceness in battle that of the lion, her glory was that of the sun shining down upon the Earth, and all the people bowed down before her in fear and praise.

One day, Inanna went forth into the mountains. She went to Elam and Subir. She went into the Lulubi Mountains. She went into the Lulubi Mountains, and there, in the midst of them, was the greatest peak, which was called Ebih. As Inanna passed, all the mountains bowed low before her and did her honor, but Ebih would not bend. Ebih did not bow down to the ground before her; Ebih did not kiss the dust at her feet. This greatly angered Inanna, and she swore she would have vengeance on Ebih for its disrespect.

"Truly shall I make Ebih know my wrath! Truly shall I make it know how it has wronged me! Ebih did not bow down before me, and Ebih did not kiss the dust at my feet. I shall bring battle to the mountains. I shall bring my battering ram and my bow and quiver of arrows. I shall bring my lance and my shield. Fire will I bring to the forests of the mountains and an axe to the boles of its trees. All the mountains shall quail before my rage, and never more shall Ebih hold its head up with pride."

And so, Inanna, daughter of Nanna, put on her garments of battle and her radiant crown whose brilliance was terror to all who beheld it. She took up her seven-headed weapon and put on her sandals of lapis lazuli. When the sun had set, she went to the Gate of Wonder dressed in all her battle array. There she made an offering to An and prayed to him.

An saw Inanna and saw that she was arrayed for battle. He heard her prayer, and he smiled upon her. An sat on his divine throne, and then Inanna came forth to speak to him. "O my father, greetings! You have given me many gifts, and so it is that none can rival me in heaven or on Earth. I am terrible to behold, and none may best me in battle! I am sword and arrow, lance and shield! Kings call upon me, and I answer, and with my aid, they slay their enemies, and thus I bring glory to the name of An.

"Today I went forth into the mountains, and the mountain Ebih did me no honor. The mountain Ebih did not fear me. It did not bow down before me and kiss the dust at my feet. And so it is that I come before you, O Father An, to say that I shall go into the mountains and bring battle to them. I shall use my battering ram and my bow and arrows. I shall use my lance and my shield. Fire will I bring to the mountains and an axe to the boles of its trees. All the mountains shall quail before my rage, and never more shall Ebih hold its head up with pride.

"Let me go forth in battle array. Let me lay low the mountain that refused me the honor I am due. Let me vanquish it, and teach it to respect the goddess Inanna."

An heard the words of Inanna and said, "So you wish to destroy this mountain. Very well, but do you know what task lies before you? What do you really know of this mountain? Let me tell you what task lies before you, this task against a mountain that even the Annunaki have cause to fear. The forests of this mountain are thick, and its orchards heavy with fruit. Under the trees dwell lions, on its flanks dwell wild rams, and stags run through its meadows, where herds of wild bulls graze. This mountain is most fearsome, and you will not be able to vanquish it."

The lady Inanna did not heed the words of An. She strode away from him and pushed open the great gate of the House of the Gods. She strode through the gate in her battle array, her weapons in her hands, and her wrath was terrible to behold. Her wrath was like a great flood, and she called up a whirlwind to rage alongside her.

Inanna went into the mountains, and she brought battle to Ebih. The mountain fought fiercely, but Inanna gave no quarter. She grabbed the neck of Ebih and roared like a lion as she stabbed its vitals with her dagger.

The body of Ebih split and crumbled. The stones of Ebih's body cracked and rolled down its flanks. The serpents who lived in its caves and crevasses spat out venom.

Inanna cursed the forests of the mountain and brought a great drought upon them. She set the forests alight, and the smoke of their burning blotted out the sun. And so it was that Inanna showed that she alone had the power and that she alone was due honor and praise.

Then Inanna spoke to the mountain she had conquered, saying, "O Ebih Mountain, you thought yourself divine because of your height. You thought yourself divine because of your beauty. You thought yourself divine because your peak brushed the very heavens, but you did not know your place. You did not bow down before me and kiss the dust at my feet. And so it is that I have vanquished you and taken all your beauty and might.

"I have vanquished you as I would have done a wild bull. I have conquered you as I would have done an elephant. Behold, now your eyes can do nothing but weep, and your heart can do nothing but mourn, and the birds that nest in what is left of you shall sing songs only of grief.

"I brought to you the terror that was the gift of Enlil to me. I brought you battle with the weapons that were the gifts of Enlil, and with my strength and my weapons, I have brought the mountain down. A palace have I built for myself, and I have given ritual objects to those who carry out the cults of the gods.

"It is I who conquered the mountain. Like a flood, I washed it away. Like a raging wind, I blew it down. I am the victor over Ebih."

Praise be to Inanna, daughter of Nanna!

Praise be to Nisaba!

Dumuzi and Enkimdu

In this myth, the sun god Utu wishes his sister, the goddess Inanna, to marry the god of shepherds, Dumuzi. Inanna herself prefers Enkimdu, the god of farmers. (Enkimdu the farmer is a character distinct from Gilgamesh's friend Enkidu.) Dumuzi is insulted by Inanna's preference; he wants to be Inanna's husband. What follows is a kind of contest between Dumuzi and Enkimdu for the hand of Inanna, in which each god states what they might bring to the marriage.

Many scholars have noted the parallels between the myth of Dumuzi and Enkimdu and the biblical story of Cain and Abel, since both stories involve a quarrel between a shepherd on the one hand and a farmer on the other, encapsulating age-old conflicts between pastoral and agricultural peoples. Unlike the biblical story, however, the Sumerian myth of Dumuzi and Enkimdu ends with the two gods becoming friends and agreeing to exchange the products of their labors with one another. Inanna eventually agrees to marry Dumuzi, but that is not shown in this story.

There was a time when the sun god Utu went to his sister Inanna and said, "O my sister, it is time that you were married. It is time that you chose a husband. I think that you should marry the god of shepherds, Dumuzi. He has many fine sheep, and his ewes drop healthy lambs in their season. The milk of his goats is the best in the land, and the butter and cheese of his sheep cannot be rivaled. He would be the best husband for you."

"I'll not wed a shepherd!" cried Inanna. "I'll not wed a shepherd and wear garments of wool. I'll not wed a shepherd, no! A farmer shall be my husband. A farmer who grows grain that waves in the wind and bows down low when it is heavy in the ear. A farmer who grows good flax for fine linen. Him will I wed!"

Dumuzi heard the words of Inanna, and he said to her, "Why? Why do you prefer the farmer over me? What does the farmer Enkimdu have that I lack? He might have a good black robe, but he can trade that to me for a black ewe. He might have a good white robe, but he can trade that to me for a white ewe. He might brew good beer, but he can trade that to me for some of my goats' milk. Bread he can give to me in exchange for milk, and lentils he can give me in exchange for cheese. He can come and dine with me, and I will even give him extra butter and extra milk!"

Then Dumuzi took his sheep down to the riverbank to graze, and he was happy there with his flock. While Dumuzi watched over his sheep, Enkimdu came to him and said, "Why do you compare yourself to me, O shepherd? What reason have we to quarrel? Your sheep graze happily here by the river; I will also let them graze on the stubble after my crops have been harvested. Your sheep drink water happily from the river; I will also let them drink from the canal that waters my land."

Dumuzi listened to the words of Enkimdu, and then he said, "O farmer, let me count you as my friend. I think we should be friends, you and I."

"That is well," said Enkimdu, "and I shall share with you my barley and lentils. And also I shall bring barley and lentils to the lady Inanna, or whatever else shall be her pleasure."

The Marriage of Martu

Martu is the Sumerian name for the Akkadian god Amurru. The name "Amurru" also refers to a nomadic people who lived in the hills rather than in the more urbanized river valleys. Modern readers may know the Amurru people as "Amorites," a Semitic-speaking nomadic tribe mentioned in the Old Testament who originated in what is now modern Syria. The Amorites did not always live in peace with Sumerian and Akkadian peoples; from time to time, the Amorites would conduct raids on settlements in the Mesopotamian lowlands. City-dwelling Sumerians and Akkadians thought of the Amorites as barbarians, but it was the Amorites who flooded into and eventually took over large parts of southern Mesopotamia starting in the 22nd century BCE and who eventually founded the first great dynasty of the city of Babylon, which became one of the most important urban centers in the ancient world.

In the myth retold below, the god Martu is a member of a nomadic tribe who find themselves in the vicinity of a city called Inab, where a festival to honor the god Numushda is about to be held. Martu wishes to marry, and when he wins a wrestling competition held in honor of Numushda, he declares that his prize will be none other than the god's own daughter, Adgarkidu. One of Adgarkidu's friends is horrified over the match, since in her eyes Martu is an unwashed, unlettered barbarian not worthy to wed the city-dwelling Adgarkidu, but Adgarkidu declares, "I shall marry Martu!" This story, therefore, represents the merging of two cultures, that of the nomadic hill-dwelling Amorites and that of the agricultural and urban settlements of the Tigris and Euphrates Valleys.

Once there was a fine city called Inab. It was well built and well appointed, and its people were prosperous. In the lands around Inab lived tribes of nomads. These nomads lived by capturing gazelles with nets, and every evening, the men would go to the center of their camp to receive their rations. By the law of their god, unmarried men received a single ration. Men with a wife but no children received double, and men with a wife and a child received triple.

Among these people was a man named Martu, who was brave, handsome, and strong. He went to receive his ration, but every time, he received a double portion, even though he was unmarried. This troubled Martu, for it meant that he was receiving more than his friends, even those who were married, since they had to share their double portion with their wives.

Martu went to his mother and said, "It is not right that I should receive a double portion even though I am unmarried. It is not right that I should receive more than my married friends do. I have a mind to take a wife. What should I do?"

Martu's mother said, "If you wish to marry, choose the woman carefully. Choose a woman you can love and cherish. Take a woman you can choose for yourself."

Martu decided to follow his mother's advice. He started looking for a woman to marry, but he found none among his own people. But soon there was to be a great festival in the city of Inab, a festival in honor of the god Numushda. Martu rejoiced at this, for he could both participate in the festival and look for a wife. "Come," Martu said to his companions, "let us go to the festival together. We will enjoy ourselves and honor the god, and perhaps I shall find a wife."

And so, Martu and his friends went to Inab for the festival. There they saw the god Numushda, who was there with his wife, Namrat, and his daughter, Adgarkidu. The celebrations were very joyous. Musicians played loudly upon drums all throughout the city, and in the temple of Numushda, the young men gathered to compete in wrestling competitions in his honor.

Martu went to the temple and entered the competition for he loved to wrestle, and he desired to honor the god as was right and proper to do. In every bout, Martu was the victor. No one could match him for strength or skill. Every one of the men who wrestled against him was defeated. Many went home wounded, and a few died, for they could not withstand Martu's great strength.

Numushda watched the wrestling competition, and he marveled at the strength and skill of Martu. When he saw that Martu had defeated all the other wrestlers, Numushda rejoiced greatly. He went to Martu and said, "Lo, you have brought me great honor this day! Let me reward you as you deserve. I shall give you much silver as your reward."

Martu bowed to the god and said, "The lord Numushda is most generous, but I do not desire silver."

"What, then?" said Numushda. "Will you accept gold? Jewels? I am rich beyond compare, and I will share my wealth with you."

"Neither gold nor jewels are my desire. I wish to marry your daughter, Adgarkidu, for I have seen her there with you, watching the competition, and my heart is given to her."

"Very well," said Numushda, "but if you are to marry her, you must pay a bride price worthy of the daughter of a god."

"Name your price, and I shall pay it," said Martu.

"My price is calves. Many calves, with their mothers to give milk, and a bull to breed with."

"That price I can pay," said Martu.

"My price also is lambs. Many lambs, with their mothers to give milk, and a fine ram to breed with."

"That price I can pay," said Martu.

"My price also is kids. Many kids, with their mothers to give milk, and a fine he-goat to breed with."

"All of your price I can pay," said Martu, "and more besides."

Martu paid the price to Numushda as he promised, and he gave many fine gifts of gold and silver to the people of Inab. Also he gave them fine garments to wear, of many colors, and shawls for the old women.

The days went by, but still the marriage feast had not been held. Adgarkidu's friend watched the preparations and saw how Martu paid his bride price, but she thought very little of Martu, despite his generosity, his strength, and his good looks. The friend went to Adgarkidu and said, "Why are you marrying that Martu? He really is not worthy of you. Don't you know that he and his people live out in the open, in tents, with only the hide of goats to keep out the wind and the rain? They roam everywhere in the wilderness, like animals. I'll wager Martu doesn't even know how to honor the gods properly. He probably knows none of the prayers and none of the rituals. I've even heard that people like him eat their meat raw! Surely you cannot think to marry Martu!"

But Adgarkidu simply looked at her friend and said, "I shall marry Martu!"

Part II: Tales of Kings and Heroes
Enmerkar and the Ensuhkeshdanna

Enmerkar was the legendary first king of Uruk, who was deified and the subject of several myths. Enmerkar is credited with having built the city of Uruk, one of the principal ancient Sumerian cities situated between the Tigris and Euphrates Rivers in what is now southern Iraq. Enmerkar also is described as the father of Lugalbanda, the legendary second king of Uruk and the grandfather of Gilgamesh, an actual historical personage whose exploits became mythologized in the ancient Epic of Gilgamesh.

Tales about Enmerkar often state that he is the son of Utu, the sun god, which also makes him a nephew to the goddess Inanna, the tutelary goddess of Uruk. In the story retold below, Enmerkar is engaged in a rivalry with Ensuhkeshdanna, the lord of Aratta, a mythical city that is described in various tales as beautiful and supremely wealthy. Here Enmerkar and Ensuhkeshdanna are fighting over which one of them is more entitled to the favors of Inanna. The two kings undertake their fight for supremacy by means of contests between their chief sorcerers.

Once there were two cities, Uruk and Aratta. Enmerkar, son of Utu, was lord over Uruk, and Ensuhkeshdanna was lord over Aratta. One day, Ensuhkeshdanna had a mind to begin a rivalry with Enmerkar, and so he summoned his messenger and said to him, "Go you to the city of Uruk, and take this message to Enmerkar. Tell Enmerkar that he should submit to me because although he might enjoy the favors of Inanna on a beautiful bed, I enjoy her on an even more splendid bed. And although Enmerkar might see her while she sleeps at night,

I see her during the day and hold converse with her. Enmerkar might have a fine flock of geese, but mine is even better, and if Enmerkar does not submit, he will have to beg me to have geese from my flock."

The messenger ran to Uruk with the swiftness of a hawk in flight and went before Enmerkar to deliver his message. "My Lord Enmerkar, Ensuhkeshdanna, lord of Aratta, begs me to tell you this: 'Enmerkar should submit to me because although he might enjoy the favors of Inanna on a beautiful bed, I enjoy her on an even more splendid bed. And although Enmerkar might see her while she sleeps at night, I see her during the day and hold converse with her. Enmerkar might have a fine flock of geese, but mine is even better, and if Enmerkar does not submit, he will have to beg me to have geese from my flock.'"

Enmerkar heard the words of the messenger from Aratta, and he said, "Take this message back to your master. Tell him that while he might lie with Inanna on his own beautiful bed, I lie with her on her own bed that is carved with figures of lions. Enlil himself made me king. When I was a baby, the mighty Ninurta dandled me on his lap, and I nursed at the breast of Aruru, sister to Enlil. Inanna might pay visits to Aratta, but it is in Uruk that she makes her home. And what of your flocks of geese? You have none. Any geese you have will be gotten from me, Enmerkar, King of Uruk."

The messenger ran swiftly back to Aratta and delivered Enmerkar's message to Ensuhkeshdanna. When Ensuhkeshdanna heard Enmerkar's words, he was downcast. "What reply ought I to make to Enmerkar? I tested him, and he bested me for sure."

Ensuhkeshdanna's counselors said, "It was you who first sent a boastful message to Uruk. You need not worry about what he will do; you need to control yourself. Stop vying with Enmerkar; you will achieve nothing good by doing that."

Ensuhkeshdanna scoffed at the advice of his counselors. "Enmerkar might raze my city to the ground, and yet I will be one piece of brick amongst the rubble. I will never submit to the King of Uruk."

Word of the contest between Ensuhkeshdanna and Enmerkar came to the ears of a sorcerer named Urgirinuna, a man from Hamazu. He had come to live in Aratta after his own city was destroyed. Urgirinuna went to Ensuhkeshdanna's vizier and said, "I have heard what passed between Ensuhkeshdanna and Enmerkar. Tell your lord Ensuhkeshdanna that I am a sorcerer and that I can make Uruk submit to Aratta. I can make Uruk and all of its territories bow before the might of Aratta. Enmerkar and the people of Uruk will come here, and instead of living in their own city, they will have to work for us."

The vizier told Ensuhkeshdanna what the sorcerer had said. "This is excellent!" said Ensuhkeshdanna. "Bring the sorcerer to me, that I may give him gold and silver for his journey, and tell him that if he succeeds, he shall have nothing but the choicest food to eat and nothing but the finest wine to drink for the rest of his days."

The sorcerer accepted the money from Ensuhkeshdanna and set out toward the city of Uruk. When he arrived at Uruk, city of the goddess Nisaba, he went into the cow byre. The cow trembled when she saw the sorcerer. "Who drinks your milk and eats your butter?" said the sorcerer, who had the power to speak to animals.

"Nisaba it is who drinks my milk and eats my butter. My cheese graces Nisaba's table," said the cow.

"May your milk go into your horns," said the sorcerer. "May your milk go into your back."

Next the sorcerer went to the pen where the goat was kept. The goat trembled when she saw the sorcerer.

"Who drinks your milk and eats your butter?" said the sorcerer to the goat.

"Nisaba it is who drinks my milk and eats my butter. My cheese graces Nisaba's table," said the goat.

"May your milk go into your horns," said the sorcerer. "May your milk go into your back."

When the cowherd went to milk the cow, he found that she had no milk in her udder, and her calf was crying loudly in hunger. When the goatherd went to milk the goat, he found that she had no milk either, and her kid was crying also. The cowherd and the goatherd wept in despair. They fell down on the ground and prayed to Utu. "O mighty Utu," they said, "the sorcerer from Aratta came here and made the cow and the goat stop giving milk. The animals have no milk to feed their young, and we have no milk to give to the people. Utu, grant us your aid!"

At that time, there was a wise woman named Sagburu who lived in Uruk. She heard what the sorcerer had done to the cow and the goat. "This cannot stand," she said to herself. "I must do something about that evil sorcerer."

And so Sagburu went to speak to Enmerkar. "I know who it is who has made the milk dry up," Sagburu said to the king, "and I shall make him pay for his crime."

"What will you do?" said Enmerkar.

"I shall have a contest of magic with him," she said. "I shall defeat him, and then he will pay the price for his misdeeds."

"Very well," said Enmerkar. "Your reward will be very great if you are successful. Go and challenge the sorcerer with my blessing!"

Soon enough, Sagburu found the sorcerer, who was sitting in the shade of a tree near the river. "Sorcerer!" she said. "I have heard what you did to the cow and the goat of Nisaba. Surely you shall pay for your misdeeds."

The sorcerer stood and faced Sagburu and said, "I will do no such thing. I am the mightiest sorcerer in the land, and I answer to no one, save that they can defeat me in a contest of magic."

"What if I were to accept that challenge?" said Sagburu.

"You? Accept my challenge? I think you will lose," said the sorcerer. "But if you choose defeat, that is your business. So, this is what I propose: we should each throw fish spawn into the river and make animals arise from it. If my animals defeat yours, then I win. If your animals defeat mine, then you win."

"I accept your challenge," said Sagburu.

The woman and the sorcerer each took a handful of fish spawn and threw it into the river. The sorcerer's fish spawn changed into a giant carp that leapt out of the water. The woman's fish spawn turned into an eagle that swooped down upon the carp and caught it in its talons. Then the eagle flew away into the mountains with the carp.

Again, the woman and the sorcerer threw fish spawn into the river. The sorcerer made his fish spawn turn into an ewe and its lamb. The woman made her fish spawn turn into a wolf. The wolf leapt upon the ewe and its lamb and dragged them away into the desert.

A third time they threw fish spawn into the river. The sorcerer made his fish spawn turn into a cow and its calf. The woman made her fish spawn turn into a lion. The lion leapt upon the cow and its calf and dragged them away into the reed beds.

A fourth time they threw fish spawn into the river. The sorcerer made his fish spawn turn into an ibex and a wild sheep. The woman made her fish spawn turn into a leopard. The leopard leapt upon the ibex and the wild sheep and dragged them away into the mountains.

A fifth time they threw fish spawn into the river. The sorcerer made his fish spawn turn into a gazelle kid. The woman made her fish spawn turn into a tiger and a lion. The tiger and the lion leapt upon the gazelle kid and dragged it away into the forest.

The sorcerer saw how the wise woman had defeated him every time, and he quailed. Sagburu said to him, "Sorcerer, you do have some power, but what did you think you would achieve by challenging a wise woman of Uruk? What did you think you would achieve by challenging a wise woman of the city of Nisaba, the city beloved of Ninlil, whose destiny is decreed by none other than Enlil and An?"

"Have mercy on me," said the sorcerer. "I knew nothing of this when I came to Uruk. You have won our contest; I grant that you are the more powerful magician. Please do not harm me. Let me return home to Aratta, and there I will sing your praises to all who will listen."

Sagburu replied, "You came to Uruk, and you frightened the animals. You dried up the udders of the cow and the goat, so that now we have no milk and no butter. You took away the milk, and now we have no cheese to grace our tables. There is no pardon for this offense in Uruk; the law commands it so." Then Sagburu threw the sorcerer into the river and killed him. When Sagburu was sure the sorcerer was dead, she returned home to her city.

When Ensuhkeshdanna found out what had happened to his sorcerer, he sent a messenger to Enmerkar. The messenger came before Enmerkar and said, "Ensuhkeshdanna, my master, bids me tell you this: 'Surely Enmerkar is the favored of Inanna, and you are the first in all the lands. I am not your equal and will never match you.'"

Lugalbanda in the Mountain Cave

This tale is part of a longer narrative detailing deeds of Enmerkar's heroic son, Lugalbanda, who in turn was the father of the great Gilgamesh. The pretext for this story is Enmerkar's desire to wage war on Aratta. During the march of Uruk's army through the Zabu (Zagros) Mountains on their way to Aratta, Lugalbanda is paralyzed by illness, and his friends make the heart-wrenching decision to leave him behind in the hopes that he will recover and rejoin them.

Lugalbanda's companions leave him well provisioned with many kinds of food and drink, as well as his axe and dagger. The translators of this story from the Electronic Text Corpus of Sumerian Literature note that while Lugalbanda's friends hope he will get well again, they are in fact hedging their bets and also preparing him for burial, since the kinds of items they leave with him were part of Sumerian burial traditions. The story also shows the importance of the sun, the moon, and the planet Venus within Sumerian religion, since Lugalbanda prays to each of them for healing once he recovers enough to be able to pray at all. A further point of the story is to show how important and favored Lugalbanda is, since in addition to the three deities who heal him, he is visited by Zangara, the god of dreams, and by four major deities (An, Enlil, Enki, and Ninhursag), who come to eat the offering feast he prepares for them.

There came a time when Enmerkar, King of Uruk, decided to mount a campaign against the city of Aratta. Aratta would not submit to Uruk, and so Enmerkar marshaled his army and prepared for an assault against that strong and beautiful city. The number of men in Enmerkar's army was so great that it was like a flood in numbers and in strength.

When all was ready, Enmerkar led his army on the road to Aratta. Enmerkar marched at the head of his army, and his armor and weapons glinted in the sun. So brightly did they shine that all who saw him did not wonder in the least that this was the very son of Utu. The army of Uruk marched over hills and across plains. For five days, they marched toward Aratta. On the sixth day, they stopped to rest, and on the seventh, they began to march into the mountains.

Now, the captains of Enmerkar's army were seven warriors, champions and heroes all, sons of Urash, the earth goddess, and raised in the very house of An himself. The eighth captain was Enmerkar's son, Lugalbanda, a man both strong and crafty. But while the army was marching through the mountains, Lugalbanda fell gravely ill. He fell to the ground and could neither move nor speak, although he still breathed and his heart still beat. Enmerkar's and Lugalbanda's friends all tried to help him, but nothing they did made any difference.

"We should bring him back to Uruk," said one soldier.

"We cannot," said Enmerkar, "for it is too far to go, and we can spare no one."

"Let us bring him back to Kulaba then," said another.

"We cannot," said Enmerkar, "for it is too far to go, and we can spare no one."

Lugalbanda's friends looked about the place where they had stopped, and they spied a small cave in the side of the mountain. "Let us leave him there," said one, "let us leave him there with provisions and coverings, and maybe the gods will smile upon him and heal him, and he will rejoin us when he is well."

Enmerkar agreed that this was a good plan. The soldiers placed Lugalbanda inside the cave and wrapped him well to keep him warm. They left him a good number of provisions, dates and figs and cheese, bread and butter, wine and beer, all packed into leather bags. Then they prepared some incense in a dish and suspended it from the roof of the cave above Lugalbanda's head. Then they placed his good tin axe and good iron dagger next to him, and during all these preparations, Lugalbanda's eyes were open. He watched what his friends did, and tears flowed down his cheeks, but he was still unable to move or speak.

Lugalbanda's friends said to him, "If you should get well, there is food and drink here to make you strong again. May Utu make you well and bring you home safe to your city of Kulaba. But if Utu should call you to the afterlife, we shall stop here when our business in Aratta is done, and we will bring your body home for proper burial."

Then Enmerkar's and Lugalbanda's friends left the cave, and the army marched on without him, shedding bitter tears all the while, for they all were sure that they would never see the mighty Lugalbanda alive again.

For two days did Lugalbanda lie in that cave, unable either to move or to speak. On the afternoon of the third day, he was able to move a little and speak a little, but he was still very weak and very ill. Lugalbanda raised his hands to the heavens and with many bitter tears prayed to Utu. "O Utu, O shining one, you are ever blessed! I beg you, let me be well again. Let me be well so that I can leave this cave and rejoin my friends. I do not wish to die here, alone and untended by any who care for me. I do not wish for my companions to return here only to find my dead body. O Utu, O shining one, let me be well again!"

Utu heard the prayers of Lugalbanda and spoke to him with words of encouragement, but still Lugalbanda was weak and ill.

When Utu had gone to his rest, Lugalbanda looked out into the sky, and there he saw the brightness of Inanna. Lugalbanda raised his hands to her, and with many bitter tears, he prayed. "O Inanna, O shining one! Here I am in this cave, when I should be with my friends. Here I am, alone and friendless, when I should be in my own beautiful city. Let me be well again! I pray you, O shining one, do not let me die here, alone and friendless!"

Inanna heard the prayers of Lugalbanda. She came into his cave and gave him the gift of healing sleep and the gift of peace in his heart, and then she returned to her own city.

Lugalbanda slept for a time, and when he woke, it was deep night. Lugalbanda looked out into the sky, and there he saw Nanna shining brightly. Lugalbanda lifted his hands to Nanna and with many tears prayed to him. "O bright Nanna, O shining one! Truly you love justice and despise evil! You are mighty in justice and wrathful against those who do evil! Let me be well again, O bright Nanna!"

Nanna heard Lugalbanda's prayers and saw his tears, and he gave to him the movement of his limbs. Once again, Lugalbanda was able to stand.

In the morning, Lugalbanda saw the brightness of Utu as he rose above the horizon. The light of the sun god poured into Lugalbanda's cave, and the evil god who had struck Lugalbanda down departed from him. When Lugalbanda realized he was well again, he said a prayer of thanks to Utu, praising him greatly.

Lugalbanda walked out of the cave, and there he saw healing plants growing and a stream flowing with life-giving water, the gifts of the gods to him. Lugalbanda ate of the plants and drank of the water, and all his strength returned. Rejoicing that he felt well again, Lugalbanda ran through the mountains, swift and surefooted. Then he returned to his cave and packed his weapons and the provisions his companions had left for him, and he set off to find Enmerkar and his army.

After walking for some time, Lugalbanda decided to stop and make camp. He made a fire and baked good bread in the embers. He ate the bread with date syrup. While Lugalbanda was eating, he heard the sound of a great beast tearing at the grass. He looked about him, and there he saw a huge wild bull, eating the grass and drinking from a nearby stream. Lugalbanda lay in ambush for the bull. He seized it by the horns and subdued it, then he tethered it in a place near his camp. Next a herd of goats passed near to Lugalbanda's camp. Lugalbanda went out and captured two fine goats. He seized them, subdued them, then tethered them in a place near his camp.

His meal eaten, the bull and the goats captured, Lugalbanda felt overcome with weariness. He made himself a bed of fresh mountain herbs. Then he took a drink of the good beer his friends had given him, and he lay down to sleep.

While Lugalbanda slept, he had a dream. Zangara, the very god of dreams himself, appeared to Lugalbanda in the guise of a great bull. Zangara bellowed to Lugalbanda, saying, "Who will sacrifice the wild bull for me? Who will sacrifice the wild goats for me? Who will pour out their blood in sacrifice? The one who must do this is he who wields the axe of tin. The one who must do this is he who wields the dagger of iron. Let him make an offering to the gods. Let him offer the bull and the goats to the gods at the break of day."

Lugalbanda awoke from his dream, shivering. He sat for a time in awe at the god's apparition to him. Then he took up his axe and his dagger and did as Zangara commanded. He sacrificed the bull and the goats at the break of day, pouring out their blood into a pit. Lugalbanda prepared the offerings in a banquet for the gods, and lo! Enlil, An, Enki, and Ninhursag came to dine upon the freshly roasted meat. Lugalbanda fed them well on the roasted meat and on the beer and wine he had on hand, and for a libation he poured out fresh water.

Then Lugalbanda set up altars to Nanna and Utu, and he decorated them well with lapis lazuli. For Nanna and Utu, Lugalbanda set out fresh cakes.

[What remains of the story is fragmentary, and the end of the story is lost. The parts that remain depart from a narrative about Lugalbanda and launch into what the Electronic Corpus of Sumerian Literature says is a description of demons. These descriptions pair the demons (or whoever else is being described) with various attributes that are connected to the relevant god or goddess. For example, one line calls them "gazelles of Suen," while another calls them "fine smooth cloths of Ninlil."]

Lugalbanda and the Anzu Bird

This story of the heroic exploits of Lugalbanda continues the narrative of the rivalry between Uruk and the mythical city of Aratta. It also continues the epic of Lugalbanda, explaining how he rejoins the rest of Enmerkar's army after he recovers from the illness that caused his companions to leave him behind in a cave in the Zabu (Zagros) Mountains in the hope that he might recover.

The Zagros is a range that runs from west to east along the southern edge of Turkey, turns southeastward to run along the border between Iraq and Iran, and then farther south along the eastern shore of the Persian Gulf. The Zagros range was both distant from Sumerian lands and home to peoples who occasionally were hostile to the Sumerians; thus, in Sumerian myths, these mountains are painted as a dangerous place that one might enter but not leave alive, as well as a home to strange and fantastic creatures.

One such creature that Lugalbanda encounters in his wanderings is the Anzu Bird. The Anzu Bird or, more simply, "Anzu," is a formidable creature that appears in many Sumerian and Mesopotamian tales, having aspects that are either good or evil depending on when the particular story about the bird was created. The story retold here leans toward presenting the Anzu Bird as vain and fearsome but basically good. Some representations of Anzu in ancient art show him as a lion-headed eagle and others as half-man, half-bird. The Anzu Bird was associated with thunder and storms in ancient Sumerian myths, and although considered a powerful being, it seems to have not enjoyed its own worship cult.

There came a time when Lugalbanda was on campaign with the armies of the cities of Uruk, going out to fight the city of Aratta alongside King Enmerkar, son of Utu, the sun god, and Lugalbanda became separated from his companions. Lugalbanda was lost in the Zabu Mountains and had no one to turn to for advice. As Lugalbanda walked along a mountain path, he spied the nest of the Anzu Bird, a monstrous creature with enormous talons and a serrated beak like the mouth of a shark. The nest was in a great tree, the crown of which spread out even over the highest mountain peaks, and its roots were buried in the mouth of a great river belonging to Utu, god of the sun.

"I know what I shall do," said Lugalbanda. "I shall go to the bird and speak to him graciously. I shall provide good beer and sweet cakes for him and his family. Maybe if I treat him well, he will tell me where my brothers in arms have gone, where I might find the troops of my city Uruk."

Lugalbanda made cakes, sweetening them with golden honey. He went to the Anzu Bird's nest and found inside it a young chick. Lugalbanda fed the sweet cakes to the chick, and also some meat and good sheep's fat. Then he beautified the chick, painting its eyes with kohl and perfuming it with oil of cedar. He decorated the nest with bright flowers and shavings of cedar. Leaving behind some salted meat, Lugalbanda went and hid himself, waiting to see what would happen.

While Lugalbanda fed the chick and decorated the nest, the Anzu Bird was out herding his cattle. When his work was done, he captured one of the bulls and killed it, and he laid it across his back. Then he picked up a live bull in his talons, and with his burdens, he flew home. The Anzu Bird arrived at his nest but could not see his chick inside it. When the Anzu Bird's wife arrived and looked inside the nest, she also saw the chick had gone missing. The Anzu Bird and his wife both sent up a cry of mourning. "Where has our chick gone? Oh, this is a most terrible thing. Who has taken away our precious child?"

The Anzu Bird looked more closely at his nest, and he saw that it had been decorated with bright flowers and cedar shavings, and in the midst of this was the chick, its eyes painted with kohl and its down anointed with oil of cedar. The Anzu Bird saw this and rejoiced. "Look and see! Look what has become of my nest! Surely it is now a palace for a great king. Who has done this? Come, show yourself! Enlil is my father, and I have the power to decide fates and destinies. Show yourself, and I shall make a path for you clear of all enemies and strife!"

Lugalbanda came out from his hiding place and bowed low before the great bird. "O mighty Anzu Bird, your eyes sparkle like a heaven full of stars. Your wingspan is so great the sky can barely encompass it. The sharpness of your talons is beyond compare and is the bane of bulls and cows, sheep and goats. Your feathers are more beautiful than the freshest, most well-tended garden. I came here yesterday, hoping to put myself under your protection; I greet you well and ask that you decide my fate for me."

"Your fate shall be to take away a great gift," said the Anzu Bird. "You will have a great barge full of all good things, grain and cucumbers, apples and gold. That shall be your fate."

"O great Anzu Bird," said Lugalbanda, "that is most generous, but it is not what I desire."

"Take then these arrows," said the bird. "They will always strike their target. You will be the greatest archer in the whole world!"

"O great Anzu Bird," said Lugalbanda, "surely that is a great gift, but it is not what I desire."

"Then take the mighty helmet of Ninurta and his golden breastplate."

"Ah," said Lugalbanda, "you tempt me with great honor, but alas, that is not what I desire."

"What of the butter churn of Dumuzi? It never empties, and it never tires of churning out the sweetest butter," said the bird.

"Indeed that is a fine gift," said Lugalbanda, "but it is not what I desire."

"Now, then, Lugalbanda, it is not good that you should refuse all of my gifts. But I owe you a debt, and so, I will give you whatever you ask of me."

"O great Anzu Bird," said Lugalbanda, "give me the power of running. Let me run and run and never tire! Let me run swift as the lightning, swift as the howling wind. If I look toward the place I wish to go, let me arrive there in no time! Give me this, and I shall command a statue to be made of you, more beautiful than any other statue in the world. All of Sumer shall hear of your beauty and your power, and great praise shall come to you and to the gods thereby."

And so it was that the Anzu Bird gave to Lugalbanda the power of running. He gave to him the power of running without tiring; he gave him the swiftness of the lightning and the howling wind. "And lo," said the bird, "my statue shall be the most beautiful, and my name proclaimed throughout all of Sumer!"

Lugalbanda thanked the bird well for his gift and then asked if the bird knew where his companions were. "I know not," said the bird, "but I will see whether I can find them."

The Anzu Bird spread his great wings and flew aloft. After circling for some time, he spied the troops of Uruk. He returned to his nest and said, "I have found them, Lugalbanda, and I will tell you which way to go, but first you must listen to my words. When you find your companions, do not tell them of the gift I gave you, for one never knows when a gift may turn out to be a curse in disguise. And do not return here to my nest. You stay with your friends."

Lugalbanda took up his weapons and set out to find the troops of the city of Uruk. When he arrived in their camp, they were surprised and happy to see him. "Lugalbanda!" they cried. "Where have you been? We looked for you everywhere but could not find you. We had given you up for dead! No one ever comes back from those mountains alive!"

"Well, I forded the rivers on my own two legs and drank up all their waters," said Lugalbanda. "I ate of what I found in the meadows and of the acorns beneath the trees." All the men of Uruk flocked around Lugalbanda to hear his story, to press food and drink upon him, and to rejoice that he had returned to them unharmed.

The next day, the armies of Uruk marched to the city of Aratta, and they made their encampment outside the walls. The men of Aratta hurled javelins and stones at the men of Uruk. The men of Aratta hurled so many javelins and stones that it was like rain falling from the sky.

For a long time, the men of Uruk fought to take Aratta, but they did not succeed. They tried for many months, and soon the months had turned into a year, and still Aratta did not fall. In front of them, the men of Uruk had a storm of javelins and stones, and behind them they had mountains full of thorns and fell beasts, and no one knew how they might return to their city alive.

King Enmerkar, brave as he was, began to think that maybe this was where he would meet his doom, alongside his army. He asked among his soldiers who would go back to Uruk to find aid, but none would go. He went to his elite soldiers, heroes every one of them, and asked who of them would go to Uruk, but none would go. Again, he asked the regular soldiers, and again, they refused. Once more, Enmerkar went to the elite soldiers and asked who of them would go to Uruk, and this time, Lugalbanda stood forth and said, "O King Enmerkar, I will do this errand, but I must do it alone."

Enmerkar said, "Very well. Go you to Uruk, and go without companions. Take with you the standard of Uruk. Go in haste! Return soon! Guard the standard with your very life!"

Then Enmerkar, son of Utu, said to Lugalbanda, "This is the message you shall bear. Go to my sister Inanna and say: 'O Inanna, my sister! Your wish it was that I raise the city of Uruk from out of the marsh of Uruk. The mighty Enki helped me drain the marsh, and there I built my city, and the building of it took fifty years. And now I find myself here on campaign, and my holy sister has abandoned me. You have fled back to the city of Uruk, leaving me here to lead these armies alone. If you are going to abandon me, at the very least see to it that I return home, so that I might lay aside my spear. And when I return, you may split my shield asunder.' That it what you are to say to my sister Inanna."

Then Lugalbanda left the presence of the king and went to collect what he needed for his journey. Word had spread throughout the camp that Lugalbanda was leaving on the king's errand, and everywhere he went his comrades shouted for him not to leave. "Why must you go?" they said. "Find someone else to do this errand! Do not leave us!"

"I must go," said Lugalbanda. "I made a solemn oath to the king, and I must go alone."

"If you leave you will never return," said his companions. "You must cross those mountains, and no one ever comes down from them alive!"

"I must not tarry," said Lugalbanda. "I must go, and no one must come with me."

Lugalbanda took up his weapons and provisions, and he left the camp. He walked into the mountains and across the plains. He arrived in the city of Uruk by midnight and went before the lady Inanna. Lugalbanda said to her, "O Lady Inanna, greetings. I come to you with a message from your brother, Enmerkar, who bids me say this: 'O Inanna, my sister! Your wish it was that I raise the city of Uruk from out of the marsh of Uruk. The mighty Enki helped me drain the marsh, and there I built my city, and the building of it took fifty years. And now I find myself here on campaign, and my holy sister has abandoned me. You have fled back to the city of Uruk, leaving me here to lead these armies alone. If you are going to abandon me, at the very least see to it that I return home, so that I might lay aside my spear. And when I return, you may split my shield asunder.'"

Inanna listened well to the message of Lugalbanda, and she said to him, "I thank you for bringing me my brother's words. Here is the message you must bring back to him. Tell him that he must go to the holy river of Inanna. On its banks grow the sacred tamarisk trees. One tamarisk stands alone there. Enmerkar must cut down that solitary tamarisk and make from it a bucket. Then he must clean the riverbank of its reeds and catch the holy *suhurmash* fish that swims in those waters. He must cook the fish and season it well, and then he must offer it to the holy war weapon of Inanna. When that is done, Enmerkar shall have the strength he needs to defeat the city of Aratta. And when he has taken the city, he must take from it its metal and metalworkers and its stones and stonemasons. He must rebuild the city and make it his. Enmerkar must do what I command, and then the city of Aratta shall belong to him."

The Sumerian Gilgamesh

Part I: Inanna and the Huluppu Tree

The Sumerian version of the Gilgamesh epic shares certain episodes with the later and more well-known Babylonian version, but other aspects of the Sumerian collection of tales are distinct. The story retold below is one of these distinct myths, telling of events that happened right after the creation of the world. In this story, Gilgamesh is said to be the brother of the goddess Inanna, who has planted a huluppu *tree—possibly a willow, according to Assyriologist Samuel Kramer—from which she wishes to make some furniture. But the female demon Lilith, a serpent, and the Anzu Bird are occupying the tree, preventing Inanna from cutting it down, so she enlists Gilgamesh to help her.*

Although Gilgamesh was an actual historical personage who ruled Sumer some time before circa 2300 BCE, here we see him as a mythologized hero and divine figure who can easily banish such powerful creatures as Anzu Birds and who can uproot whole trees with his bare hands. In gratitude for her brother's help, Inanna uses the branches and roots of the tree to make for Gilgamesh a mikku *and a* pukku, *two objects that are thought to have been the stick and the ball, respectively, that were used in some sort of ancient Sumerian game, the rules of which are now lost.*

Long, long ago, in the first days of the world, in those first days after all had been created by the gods, a *huluppu* tree grew by the banks of the Euphrates River. But one day, a great storm arose, a storm with a great southerly wind, and the wind uprooted the tree and sent it toppling into the water.

The tree floated along down the river. Holy Inanna was walking along the banks of the river, and she saw the tree being carried along by the current. Inanna thought to herself, "If I take this tree home and plant it in my garden in Uruk, it will grow well, and I shall use it to make a fine chair for me to sit upon and a fine couch for me to lie upon."

And so Inanna plucked the tree from the river and then planted it in her garden. Inanna tended the tree well and carefully, waiting for it to grow large enough that she could use it to make her chair and her couch.

After many years, the tree had grown tall, and its trunk had grown thick, and so Inanna thought to cut down the tree, for now it might make a fine chair and a fine couch. But when Inanna tried to cut down the tree, she found that she could not do it. Inanna could not cut down the tree, for a serpent that no magic could touch had twined itself around the trunk at the roots, and the Anzu Bird had made a nest for its young in the branches, and the demon-woman Lilith had made her home inside the trunk.

Inanna saw the serpent and the bird and the woman who had made their homes in her tree, and Inanna wept. She wept many bitter tears, this woman who had known only joy until now. She wept because she could not cut down her tree and make either her fine chair or her fine couch.

Inanna went to her brother, Utu, the god of the sun. She told him all that had happened, how she plucked the tree from the river and planted it in her garden, how she wanted to make a chair and a couch from its wood, but that now she could not cut down the tree because of the serpent and the Anzu Bird and the demon-woman Lilith.

Utu did not listen to his sister. He refused to help Inanna.

Inanna went to her brother, Gilgamesh, the mighty hero. She told him all that had happened, how she plucked the tree from the river and planted it in her garden, how she wanted to make a chair and a couch from its wood, but that now she could not cut down the tree because of the serpent and the Anzu Bird and the demon-woman Lilith.

The mighty Gilgamesh helped his sister, Inanna. Gilgamesh strapped on his armor and took up his mighty axe that he had wielded against many enemies, the armor and the axe that no other man had the strength to bear or wield. Then Gilgamesh summoned his companions from the city of Uruk, and together with his companions, Gilgamesh went to the tree his sister had planted in her garden.

Gilgamesh went to the tree, and he smote the serpent that could not be charmed by magic that had twined itself around the base of the tree. When the Anzu Bird saw what Gilgamesh had done to the serpent, she called to her young, and they all flew away to a far-off land. When the demon-woman Lilith saw what Gilgamesh had done to the serpent, she fled the tree and ran far, far away into the wilderness.

Then Gilgamesh uprooted the tree using nothing but his bare hands and the strength of his arms. Then the companions of Gilgamesh stripped the tree of its branches and tied them neatly into bundles. The trunk of the tree Gilgamesh gave to his sister, Inanna, and from that wood Gilgamesh made her chair and her couch. The roots and the branches of the tree Gilgamesh kept for himself. From the roots, Inanna made for Gilgamesh a *pukku*, and from the branches, she made a *mikku*, the ball and the stick that Gilgamesh used to play his game.

Part II: Enkidu in the Underworld

The greater part of this section of the myth is devoted to a detailed explication of the Sumerian understanding of the afterlife. In the Sumerian Underworld, the fortunate dead are the ones who had many children, especially sons (seven is the perfect number), while those who refused or were unable to produce children become trapped in loops of trivial annoyances. Other fortunate dead are those whose living relatives make offerings to them, as well as the stillborn children, who enjoy a sort of paradise. The lepers, on the other hand, receive no relief from their sufferings, and the warriors killed in battle must exist without comfort, knowing that their loved ones weep for them.

This section of the Sumerian Gilgamesh also varies highly from the Babylonian version in the character of Enkidu. In the Babylonian epic, Enkidu is a hairy wild man sent to kill Gilgamesh but who ends up becoming Gilgamesh's companion in arms and best friend;

together, the pair share many heroic adventures. Here in the Sumerian version, however, Enkidu is just as human and just as civilized as his noble master is, and instead of being a heroic figure, he is simply a servant, albeit one whom Gilgamesh loves very deeply.

Gilgamesh took up his *mikku* and *pukku* that he made from the wood of Inanna's *huluppu* tree and then went into the town square and began to play at ball with them. The young men of the town joined him at his game. Together they played, up and down the square. Gilgamesh did not treat the young men kindly. He hit them with the ball; he struck them with his stick. When the widows came to bring food to their sons, the young men complained that Gilgamesh had used them very roughly. When the maidens came to bring water to their brothers, the young men complained that Gilgamesh had hurt them with the violence of his play.

At sunset, Gilgamesh took his stick and marked the last spot where the ball had fallen, thinking to resume the game the next day. He took his stick and ball home, where he had a meal and retired for the night. The next morning, Gilgamesh went back to the town square to play at ball. But the widows and the young maidens had been crying to the gods about how their young men had been treated, and so, Gilgamesh's stick and ball fell out of his hands and went down, down, down into the very Underworld itself.

Gilgamesh tried to get his stick and ball back. Down, down, down he stretched his hand, but he could not reach them. He tried with his foot. Down, down, down he stretched his foot, but he still could not reach his stick and his ball. Gilgamesh went down to the Gate of the Underworld. He sat himself down in front of the gate and began to weep. "Oh, how my heart sorrows for the loss of my stick! Oh, how my eyes weep for the loss of my ball! How will I ever get them back?"

And so it was that Gilgamesh sat before the Gate of the Underworld and mourned the loss of his *mikku* and *pukku*.

Enkidu, the servant of Gilgamesh, heard his master weeping. Enkidu went to Gilgamesh and said, "O my Master, why do you weep so? What has happened that you are in mourning?"

Gilgamesh answered, "My ball and stick have fallen into the Underworld, and I cannot get them back."

"Never fear," said Enkidu. "Weep no more. I will go to the Underworld myself. I will bring back to you your stick and your ball."

"Very well," said Gilgamesh. "Go and fetch them for me. But you must listen to my instructions, and heed them well. Do not wear clean garments. The dead will know you do not belong among them. Do not anoint yourself with oil. The dead will smell the scent and surround you. Do not hurl a throwing stick in the Underworld. Those whom you strike also will surround you. Carry no staff, for that will frighten the spirits and anger them. Neither wear sandals upon your feet, nor speak with a loud voice. Embrace not the wife and son you love. Do not strike a blow upon the wife and son you hate. If they cry out, you will never be allowed to leave!

"The mother of Ninazu is there, the mother of the god of the Underworld. She is a most fearsome creature, one to be avoided, for she wears neither bright garments nor fair linen shifts, and her nails are as long and as sharp as the head of a pickaxe, and she uses these to pluck out her own hair, which grows from her head as leeks grow in a garden!"

But Enkidu did not heed the commands of Gilgamesh. He dressed himself in clean garments and anointed himself with oil. He put his sandals on his feet. He took with him his throwing stick and his staff. And there in the Underworld he hurled the throwing stick and struck some of the dead with it. He spoke with a loud voice. He embraced the wife and son he loved, and he struck the wife and son he hated. Oh, how the cry went up in the Underworld that an intruder was among the spirits of the dead and was using them ill!

Seven days went by. Gilgamesh waited for seven days for his servant Enkidu to return to him, but Enkidu did not return. Gilgamesh began to weep. "Woe, woe, woe! My beloved servant Enkidu has gone into the Underworld and cannot get out."

Gilgamesh went to the E-kur, to the home of the great god Enlil. Gilgamesh knelt before the great Enlil and said, "Woe! My beloved servant Enkidu has gone into the Underworld to fetch me back my *mikku* and *pukku*, but they will not let him out. They will not let him leave the Underworld. Enkidu has ridden through the rage of battle and did not die, yet now he is in the Underworld and cannot leave. He went into the Underworld through its own gate of his own accord. He was not brought there by Namtar, god of fate, or by the demon Asag, or even by Nergal, the god of the Underworld. Enkidu went of his own accord and now cannot leave!"

But Enlil would not hear the prayer of Gilgamesh. Enlil would not release Enkidu from the Underworld.

Next Gilgamesh went to Eridu, the home of the great god Enki. Gilgamesh knelt before the great Enki and said, "Woe! My beloved servant Enkidu has gone into the Underworld to fetch me back my *mikku* and *pukku*, but they will not let him out. They will not let him leave the Underworld. Enkidu has ridden through the rage of battle and did not die, yet now he is in the Underworld and cannot leave. He went into the Underworld through its own gate of his own accord. He was not brought there by Namtar, god of fate, or by the demon Asag, or even by Nergal, the god of the Underworld. Enkidu went of his own accord and now cannot leave!"

Enki listened to the plight of Gilgamesh, and he heard his prayer. Enki turned to his son Utu and said, "You will help Gilgamesh get his servant back. Use your power to make a crack in the Underworld. Bring back Enkidu through this crack."

Utu did what Enki commanded. He caused a great crack to form in the wall of the Underworld. Utu sent a strong wind through the crack. The wind searched out Enkidu and brought him back to the land of the living through the crack Utu had made.

When Enkidu came back to Gilgamesh, Gilgamesh embraced him heartily. Enkidu embraced his master heartily. They both wept tears of joy that Enkidu had come back alive from the Underworld.

"Tell me," said Gilgamesh, "tell me all you saw and heard in the Underworld. Tell me what it is like there, in the land of the dead."

"I can tell you these things," said Enkidu, "but you should sit down first, for surely what I have to tell will make you weep."

"Very well," said Gilgamesh, "I shall sit and weep, only tell me all."

"The organs of generation, the male member and the woman's secret place, are all rotted and turned to dust."

"Oh!" cried Gilgamesh, and then he sat down and began to weep.

"But what of the man who has one son?" said Gilgamesh. "Tell me how it goes with him in the Underworld."

"He looks at the peg that is in the wall next to him, and it makes him weep."

"And the man who has two sons? What of him?"

"He sits on some bricks and eats bread," said Enkidu.

"What of the man who has three sons? How does it go with him?"

"He drinks water that is kept in a waterskin, the sort one hangs on one's saddle," said Enkidu.

Then Gilgamesh asked, "And the man who has four sons, what happens with him in the Underworld?"

"Oh, that man rejoices, just like a man who owns four fine asses to work for him."

"What of the man who has five sons?" asked Gilgamesh.

Enkidu answered, "That man is like a good scribe. He is tireless and always may enter the palace with great ease."

"How does it go with the man who has six sons?"

"That man rejoices as does the farmer who has good land to till," said Enkidu.

"And the man who has seven sons," said Gilgamesh. "How does it go with him?"

"Oh, that man is most blessed," said Enkidu, "for he has leave to sit among the gods and listen to their speech."

"What of the man who has no sons at all?" asked Gilgamesh.

Enkidu replied, "That man must eat bread so hard that it is like a clay tile."

"And the eunuch who serves the king, what of him?"

"He stands in the corner like a useless stick."

"What of the woman who never bore children? How does it go with her?" asked Gilgamesh.

"She is cast aside like an empty pot, and no man ever approaches her."

"And the man who never had relations with his wife," said Gilgamesh. "What of him?"

"He makes a rope, and when it is done, he weeps over it," said Enkidu.

"What of the wife who never had relations with her husband?" asked Gilgamesh.

"She makes a reed mat, and when it is made, she weeps over it."

"And the lepers, how do they fare in the land of the dead?"

"They twitch like oxen do under the sting of flies," said Enkidu.

"What of the warrior who was slain on the field? What becomes of him?"

"His mother cannot comfort him, and his wife weeps without ceasing."

"The dead ones who receive no offerings," said Gilgamesh. "What becomes of them?"

"They live by gleaning crusts of bread thrown into the street by others."

"The little children who are stillborn and have died without even being named, what becomes of them?"

"Oh, they live very well, eating milk and honey off a golden table."

"And the man who was burned to death," said Gilgamesh, "what becomes of him?"

"His spirit is not in the Underworld. It went up into the sky like a wisp of smoke."

Part III: Gilgamesh and Huwawa

Despite his semi-divine nature, Gilgamesh is aware of his own mortality, and here in this story, he wishes to ensure that his name will be known after his death. In his quest to achieve this, he goes to the Mountains of Cedar to cut down trees and there disturbs a powerful and mysterious creature known as Huwawa. Huwawa is not described in the Sumerian version of the myth, but in the Babylonian version—in which he is called Humbaba—he is drawn as a kind of grotesque lion-faced giant whom the god Enlil has charged with protecting the cedar forests.

In this story, Huwawa finds the noise of Gilgamesh's logging activities to be unbearable and thus puts the hero and his companions into an enchanted sleep, which angers Gilgamesh greatly once he awakens and realizes what Huwawa has done. Gilgamesh decides to have his revenge, first by tricking Huwawa into giving Gilgamesh some of his powers. Then Gilgamesh assaults Huwawa and takes him captive, after which Enkidu kills him. In the end, Gilgamesh learns a hard lesson about vengeance and the thirst for power; when Enlil finds out what Gilgamesh and Enkidu have done, he strips Gilgamesh of Huwawa's powers and distributes them throughout the world.

One day, Gilgamesh looked toward the mountains. He looked toward the mountains where the Living One dwelled and thought to himself that he ought to make a journey there. Gilgamesh said to his servant Enkidu, "I have a mind to make a journey to the mountain of the Living One, for death comes to every man regardless of his station. I shall make a journey to that mountain and there shall I establish my name. In places where others have established their names, I also will establish mine. In places where no names have yet been established, I will establish the names of the gods."

Enkidu said, "My lord, a journey to the mountain surely is a good thing, but first you should tell Utu what you purpose to do. Tell Utu, the god of the sun, that you purpose to go to the Mountains of Cedar because all that concerns the mountains concerns Utu. Tell him what you purpose to do."

Gilgamesh saw the wisdom of Enkidu's words, and so, he took up a kid goat and held it to his breast. He took up his sacred staff and held it before his face, and then he spoke to Utu, who dwells in the heavens: "O Utu, O shining one, I purpose to go to the Mountains of Cedar. O Utu, who dwells in the heavens, I am going to the mountains, and I ask your aid!"

Utu replied, "What would you do there in the mountains? In your own land you are a king and a nobleman, but what station would you have in the mountains?"

"O shining one, I have given thought to this. I have given thought to my journey, and I wish you to attend to my thought. I look about my city, and every day people are dying. People die, and then the living mourn them, and all hearts are heavy. I looked over my city wall, I looked at the river, and lo! it was swollen with corpses. I looked over my city wall and saw that, and I know that one day I will be as one of those dead who float in the river. No man may escape his fate, for no man is great enough to achieve this.

"I know that I will die someday. I will die and I will go from this world, but before I do, I wish to establish my name in the mountains. I will establish my name in all places it can be established, and in places where no man's name may be established, I shall establish the names of the gods."

And so it was that Gilgamesh told Utu what he proposed to do, shedding many tears all the while. Utu heard the words of Gilgamesh and saw his tears and accepted those tears as a gift, as one with a compassionate heart always ought to do.

"Let me tell you what I shall do," Utu said to Gilgamesh. "I will help you in your quest. Seven warriors there are, all sons of the same mother. Great and strong are they, one and all! The eldest has a lion's paws and an eagle's talons. The second is a venomous serpent. The third is verily a dragon. The fourth is all made of flame. The fifth is yet another serpent. The sixth is a flood that washes all before him. The seventh is lightning, and none may turn him aside. There is no place on Earth that they do not know, no way or path that is unknown to them, and they will help you on your journey to the Mountains of Cedar."

Gilgamesh rejoiced greatly at the words of Utu. He went into the center of his city and blew a great blast upon his horn. The blast was so great that all who heard it wondered how one man could make such a sound, for it was so loud it sounded as though two men were blowing their horns together with all their might.

Then Gilgamesh said to the people of his city, "I require fifty men to aid me in my quest! Let them be young men and strong, who have not yet married!"

The people followed the commands of Gilgamesh. Fifty young, strong, unmarried men came forward to be the companions of Gilgamesh.

Gilgamesh led the band of fifty to the forge. There he had weapons cast for his men, long knives and battle axes. Then he led his band of fifty to the forest. There they cut down trees of ebony, apricot, and box, and they used the wood for the shafts and hilts of the weapons.

When all was ready, Gilgamesh set out for the mountains. He went to the mountains looking for the perfect cedar tree to use. He crossed the first mountain range, but the perfect cedar was not there. He crossed the second mountain range, but the perfect cedar was not there. He crossed the third mountain range, and the fourth, but the perfect cedar was not there either. He crossed the fifth mountain range, and the sixth, but the perfect cedar was not there. Finally, he came to the seventh mountain range, and there was the perfect cedar, the one Gilgamesh had been seeking.

Gilgamesh took up his mighty axe and felled that great cedar. Enkidu took up his axe and lopped off the branches. The fifty men of Gilgamesh's band picked up the branches and set them neatly in a pile.

The felling of the tree and the lopping and stacking of the branches made a great deal of noise. The noise disturbed Huwawa in his lair. Huwawa was frightened by all the noise, and so, he sent forth his power against Gilgamesh and his men. Suddenly Gilgamesh and his men were overcome with sleep. They all fell to the ground and were insensible.

For a long time they slept, and the first to wake was Enkidu. Enkidu looked about him. He rubbed his eyes and looked about, and everywhere was nothing but silence. Enkidu went to Gilgamesh and touched him, but Gilgamesh did not wake. "O Gilgamesh, O my lord and king, will you yet sleep? Look, the day is nearly ended! Utu is ending his journey and goes to his rest; will you yet sleep? The fifty who came with you, they should go back to their city. Their mothers are waiting for them. Will you yet sleep?"

But Gilgamesh would not wake, so Enkidu took a cloth and soaked it with precious oil. He rubbed the oil over the chest of Gilgamesh, and when this was done, Gilgamesh woke and jumped up on all fours like a great bull. He bent his neck downward and roared, "By the life of Ninsun, the goddess who bore me, and by my father, the great Lugalbanda, how is it that I slumber like a babe, like the babe I was at the breast of Ninsun? I swear that until I find the one who did this to me, I shall not return to my city, and I care not whether that one is mortal or divine!"

Enkidu tried to soothe his master, saying, "My lord, you have not seen the one who did this, but I have! Oh, I have seen him, and he is fearsome to behold. He is a great warrior, with teeth like a dragon. I'll wager he even feasts on man-flesh as do the lions in the desert.

"Go you up into the mountains, but let me return to our city. What shall I tell your mother? Surely she will rejoice if you yet live, but if I must tell her you have died, she will mourn and weep."

"Never fear, Enkidu," said Gilgamesh, "never fear, for we will go together and we will not die, for who will stand against us? Let us go and look for the one who did this. Never fear; let us go and find him!"

But Huwawa never let anyone come nearer to him than sixty pole-lengths, and so fearsome was that creature, that whoever he set his eye upon would die. Huwawa knew that Gilgamesh and Enkidu were approaching, and he said very plainly, "I know you are there! Never shall you return to your city! Never shall you return to your mother!"

Gilgamesh heard the words of Huwawa, and a great wave of terror rose within his body, and he found he could not move. Gilgamesh was filled with fear, and he stood as one rooted to the spot.

Huwawa looked upon Gilgamesh and said, "Look at you, so well made in your body. A beautiful son you are to your mother! A tall tree you are, noble and brave, and the apple of the gods' eyes! Put your hands on the ground, then, don't be afraid!"

Gilgamesh did as Huwawa told him to do, and with his hands on the ground, he said, "By my mother Ninsun, the goddess who bore me, and by my father, the great Lugalbanda! I think you and I should make a pact together. Let me give you my big sister Enmebaragesi to be your wife. Let me also give you my little sister Peshtur to be your concubine! They are yours if you give me your power of fear, and we shall be bound together as kinsmen."

And so, Huwawa gave to Gilgamesh his first power of fear. Gilgamesh's companions took it and stripped off the branches from it. Then they stacked the branches neatly and bound them in bundles and took them all to the foot of the mountain, where they laid them down.

Then Gilgamesh went a second time to Huwawa and said, "By my mother Ninsun, the goddess who bore me, and by my father, the great Lugalbanda! I think you and I should make a pact together. Let me give you *[text lost]*. It is yours if you give me your power of fear, and we shall be bound together as kinsmen."

And so, Huwawa gave to Gilgamesh his second power of fear. The fifty men in Gilgamesh's band lopped off all of its branches. They stacked the branches neatly and bound them in bundles and took them all to the foot of the mountain, where they laid them down.

A third time Gilgamesh went to Huwawa and said, "By my mother Ninsun, the goddess who bore me, and by my father, the great Lugalbanda! I think you and I should make a pact together. Let me give you some of the finest flour there is and the freshest, coolest water in a waterskin. They are yours if you give me your power of fear, and we shall be bound together as kinsmen."

And so, Huwawa gave to Gilgamesh his third power of fear. The fifty men in Gilgamesh's band lopped off all of its branches. They stacked the branches neatly and bound them in bundles and took them all to the foot of the mountain, where they laid them down.

Again, Gilgamesh went to Huwawa and said, "By my mother Ninsun, the goddess who bore me, and by my father, the great Lugalbanda! I think you and I should make a pact together. Here I have some beautiful big sandals for big feet. They are yours if you give me your power of fear, and we shall be bound together as kinsmen."

And so, Huwawa gave to Gilgamesh his fourth power of fear. The fifty men in Gilgamesh's band lopped off all of its branches. They stacked the branches neatly and bound them in bundles and took them all to the foot of the mountain, where they laid them down.

A fifth time Gilgamesh went to Huwawa and said, "By my mother Ninsun, the goddess who bore me, and by my father, the great Lugalbanda! I think you and I should make a pact together. Here I have some beautiful small sandals for small feet. They are yours if you give me your power of fear, and we shall be bound together as kinsmen."

And so, Huwawa gave to Gilgamesh his fifth power of fear. The fifty men in Gilgamesh's band lopped off all of its branches. They stacked the branches neatly and bound them in bundles and took them all to the foot of the mountain, where they laid them down.

Yet again Gilgamesh went to Huwawa and said, "By my mother Ninsun, the goddess who bore me, and by my father, the great Lugalbanda! I think you and I should make a pact together. Here I have some semi-precious stones, chalcedony and lapis lazuli, and some rock crystal besides. They are yours if you give me your power of fear, and we shall be bound together as kinsmen."

And so, Huwawa gave to Gilgamesh his sixth power of fear. The fifty men in Gilgamesh's band lopped off all of its branches. They stacked the branches neatly and bound them in bundles and took them all to the foot of the mountain, where they laid them down.

A seventh time Gilgamesh went to Huwawa. A seventh time Gilgamesh traded goods for Huwawa's power of fear. And so it was that Gilgamesh captured all seven of Huwawa's powers, and each time Gilgamesh took one, he would step a little closer to Huwawa, until he was standing right in front of him. When he was close enough, Gilgamesh made as if to give Huwawa a kiss but instead took his fist and punched Huwawa hard, right in the face, knocking him down.

Huwawa scowled and bared his teeth at Gilgamesh, but before he could rise, Gilgamesh threw a rope about him just as if Huwawa were a wild bull. Gilgamesh tied Huwawa up with the rope.

"You have played me false!" cried Huwawa. "You have tricked me, and you do me wrong by binding me thus!"

Gilgamesh took the end of the rope and dragged Huwawa out of his lair. "Sit down!" said Gilgamesh.

Huwawa sat down and began to weep. He wept and pleaded with Gilgamesh. "Let me go! Oh, please, set me free! Let me speak to Utu, god of the sun! O Utu, O shining one, well you know that I never knew my mother or father. Well you know that I was born here in the mountains and that you were the one who reared me. Well you know that Gilgamesh took an oath to me, swearing by heaven and by Earth and by these mountains."

Huwawa went on his knees before Gilgamesh. He prostrated himself before Gilgamesh, begging for his mercy.

Gilgamesh saw the wretchedness of Huwawa and took pity on him. Gilgamesh turned to Enkidu and said, "Let him go! We should not keep him captive. Let him go!"

But Enkidu replied, "What is this you say, O noble Gilgamesh, my king and my lord? What is this you say, O Gilgamesh, raging bull of battle, beautiful son of your mother? What is this you say, O Gilgamesh, beloved by all the people of your city of Uruk? How is it that you could be so fortunate and so noble and yet understand nothing? If you let him go free, you will never again see your beloved city! If you let him go free, he will see to it that you never return home!"

Then Huwawa said to Enkidu, "Why do you say these things? Why do you speak ill of me to him?"

When Enkidu heard this, he was overcome with rage and cut off Huwawa's head. They put Huwawa's head in a leather bag and went before Enlil with it. They prostrated themselves before Enlil and kissed the ground at his feet then upended the bag so that Huwawa's head spilled out.

Enlil saw the head of Huwawa and was displeased. "Why have you done this thing? You had no orders to kill him. You should have treated him well. You should have shared your bread and your water with him. You should have held him in honor."

Enlil took the seven powers of fear away from Gilgamesh. The first one he gave to the fields. The second one he gave to the rivers. The third went to the reeds in their beds beside the rivers. The lions received the fourth, and the fifth Enlil gave to the forests. The sixth Enlil gave to the palace, and the seventh he gave to Nungal, goddess of prisoners. All the rest of Huwawa's powers of fear Enlil kept for himself.

Part IV: Gilgamesh and Aga

If the wrath of Gilgamesh is on full display in the story of his encounter with Huwawa, here we see his mercy. When Aga, King of Kish, decides to attack Uruk, Gilgamesh defends his city well, as a king ought to do. But of course no army is strong enough to take on Gilgamesh and win, and the outcome of Aga's siege is the defeat of his army and Aga's own captivity. However, Gilgamesh remembers a time when Aga took him in and gave him hospitality, so instead of retribution, Gilgamesh gives Aga his freedom, as repayment for Aga's kindness.

Like Gilgamesh, Aga seems to have been a historical personage. Enmebaragesi, Aga's father, has been identified as an actual King of Kish, suggesting that Aga likely existed as well, and the father and son were the last two kings of the First Dynasty of Kish. (This apparently is not the same Enmebaragesi that Gilgamesh mentions as his sister in the story of Gilgamesh and Huwawa.) Enmebaragesi and Aga seem to have ruled Kish around 2600 BCE, although stories about them entered into the realm of myth sometime after their reigns ended. Kish was located between the Tigris and Euphrates Rivers in what is now central Iraq.

There was a time when Aga, son of Enmebaragesi, was king in Kish, and Gilgamesh, son of Lugalbanda, was king in Uruk. Aga sent his envoys to Uruk, demanding that Gilgamesh submit to him. Gilgamesh called together the elders of the city and the advisors to the king that he might have counsel of them. "We have yet work to be completed here," said Gilgamesh. "There are wells yet to be deepened and others yet to be dug. We should not submit to Kish. Let us bring battle to them instead."

But the elders and advisors all said, "Yes, we have work yet to be completed. We have wells yet to be deepened and others yet to be dug, but this is all the more reason to submit to Kish. We should not bring battle to them."

Gilgamesh was displeased with the words of the elders and advisors, so he went before the men of his city and said, "Envoys from Kish have come and demanded we submit to them. But we have yet work to be completed here. There are wells yet to be deepened and others yet to be dug. Never have we submitted to Kish. So, I ask you, should we bring battle to them instead?"

The men of the city answered, "Who wants to dance attendance on a foreign lord? Surely we do not. We should never submit to Kish! We should bring battle to them instead! Uruk was fashioned by the gods themselves, and Gilgamesh is its king. Gilgamesh is king and warrior, beloved of Father An! The armies of Aga have no hope of victory. They have not enough warriors, and those they do have lack courage. They shall never stand against us."

When Gilgamesh heard the reply of the men of the city, he rejoiced. Gilgamesh went to his servant Enkidu and said, "Make ready for battle! Forge weapons, construct armor! You will take up your mace, and I shall put on my radiant battle gear! Aga stands no chance against us. He will see us and quail, and we will be victorious!"

And so it was that not even five days had passed before Aga brought his armies to Uruk and laid siege to the city, and it went hard with Uruk. Gilgamesh spoke to the warriors of Uruk, saying, "An emissary we must have, someone to go to Aga. Who has the courage?"

Bihartura, one of Gilgamesh's royal guards, spoke up. "I will go! I will go to Aga, and because of me, he will quail before Uruk, and we will be victorious!"

The gate of Uruk was opened, and Bihartura passed through. But he did not get far; the men of Kish were waiting there for him. They captured Bihartura and beat him soundly from head to toe. The men of Kish bound Bihartura and brought him before Aga. Bihartura spoke with the King of Kish, but before he could finish, Aga pointed to the walls of Uruk and said, "Who is that there on the ramparts? Is that your king?"

Bihartura looked and saw that one of the officers of the army of Uruk was on the ramparts.

"That is not my king," said Bihartura. "If it were my king, you would know it. If it were my king, you would quail in fear before him. If it were my king, a multitude would fall before him and yet another multitude arise to greet him. If it were my king, all nations would bow before him, and Aga, King of Kish, would be bound and brought before him as a captive."

At these words, the men of Kish beat Bihartura again from head to toe. While they were thus beating him, Gilgamesh went to the top of the walls of Uruk and stood upon the rampart. All in the city who saw him marveled at his glory. Gilgamesh ordered that the men of the city be given maces, and then he placed them at the ready behind the city gate. The gate opened, but Gilgamesh held the men back, sending Enkidu through the gate alone.

In the camp of Kish, Aga saw Gilgamesh upon the ramparts, and he said to Bihartura, "Is that man your king?"

"Yes," said Bihartura, "that is my king."

And so it was that what Bihartura had said of Gilgamesh came true. A multitude fell before him while yet another multitude rose up to greet him. The nations bowed before him, and Aga, King of Kish, was bound and brought before Gilgamesh as a captive.

Gilgamesh looked upon Aga and said, "You treated me with kindness when I was in need. You took me in and kept me safe when I was a fugitive. I therefore repay that debt, here in the sight of Utu." And with that, Gilgamesh set Aga free to return to his own country.

When the army of Uruk saw the way Gilgamesh treated Aga, they cried out, "Praise to the lord of Uruk! Praise to the one who keeps fast the walls built by An himself!"

Sargon and Ur-Zababa

Unlike Lugalbanda and Enmerkar, who cannot be proven to have been actual kings of Sumer, Sargon of Akkad was a historical personage and the founder of the first empire in Mesopotamia, often called the Akkadian Empire. Sargon's exploits are well attested in history, but he also became the subject of legends. One such legend has to do with the mystery of his origins: like the biblical Moses, Sargon supposedly was set adrift on a river in a basket of rushes and then raised as a son by the man who found him.

Among Sargon's conquests was the land of Sumer, and so tales about Sargon exist in Sumerian as well as Akkadian sources. The Sumerian story retold below explains Sargon's initial rise to power as the successor to Ur-Zababa, who was King of Kish, a Sumerian city-state located between the Tigris and Euphrates Rivers in what is now central Iraq. In this tale, Sargon has already achieved the high status of cupbearer to the king. But the fall of Ur-Zababa has already been decided by the gods, An and Enlil, and so Sargon receives divine assistance from the goddess Inanna in his rise to power. As such, this story is part of a greater ancient tradition of mythography as a tool of propaganda legitimizing a leader's rule.

One important part of the story's plot has to do with Ur-Zababa's attempt to get rid of Sargon by sending him to a blacksmith on an errand that is supposed to lead to Sargon's demise. The means by which Sargon was to be killed is not immediately clear to modern readers; in the collection of Sumerian literature translated by Assyriologist Jeremy Black and others, Ur-Zababa orders that Sargon and a bronze mirror are to be thrown "into the mould [sic] like statues." I have taken that description to indicate that Sargon was to have been put into a mold used to cast bronze and then killed by having molten metal poured on top of him.

The great city of Kish was ruled by Ur-Zababa. A beautiful city was Kish, and a prosperous one, surrounded by fertile fields watered by many well-tended canals. But the reign of Ur-Zababa was about to come to a close, for An and Enlil had decreed that he should no longer rule over the city.

One of the workers at the royal palace of Kish was a man named Sargon. His duty was to oversee deliveries of goods to the palace. He did his duties thoroughly and well, so well, in fact, that the king appointed Sargon as the royal cupbearer, a position of great trust and importance.

There came a time when Ur-Zababa went to his rest. He slept in his royal bed, and while he was sleeping, he had a dream. When he woke, he understood what the dream was about. It troubled him, but he did not tell anyone about it. Five days passed after the dream, but not more than ten, and King Ur-Zababa became frightened and unwell. He became afflicted with a disease of the bladder. He could not contain his urine, and what passed had blood and pus in it.

While Ur-Zababa was thus afflicted, Sargon went to his bed one night, and he also had a dream. He dreamed of the goddess Inanna. In Sargon's dream, the goddess took King Ur-Zababa and drowned him in a river of blood. The goddess said to Sargon, "I am doing this for you." It was a terrifying dream, and Sargon writhed and groaned in his sleep.

Other people in the palace heard Sargon's groans, and they told the king about them. The king then called Sargon into his presence and said, "Why were you groaning in the night?"

"I was having a bad dream, O mighty Ur-Zababa," said Sargon.

"Tell me of this dream," said the king.

"As you wish, my king," said Sargon. "I dreamed of a young woman. She was the most beautiful I had ever seen. She was so tall her head reached to the heavens. She was so strong she was like the great wall of a city, broad and immovable. The woman drowned you in a river of blood. She told me she did that for me."

Ur-Zababa heard the dream of Sargon and became even more frightened than before. He crafted a plan to rid himself of Sargon. First, he called to himself Belishtikal, the chief smith. Ur-Zababa said to the smith, "That cupbearer of mine has had a dream of ill omen. He dreamed that the lady Inanna drowned me in a river of blood. I want to rid myself of Sargon. I shall send him to your smithy on an errand. I shall give him my bronze mirror and tell him to take it to you at your smithy in the E-sikil, the House of Purity, to be repaired. When Sargon arrives, throw him and the mirror alike into a mold for casting bronze. Pour molten bronze on top of them. Make a statue of it. Then no one shall be the wiser about the death of the cupbearer."

Belishtikal returned to the E-sikil and made the mold as the king had commanded him. Then Ur-Zababa called Sargon to him. He handed

Sargon the small bronze mirror and said, "Take this to the smith Belishtikal at the E-sikil. It needs to be repaired."

Sargon took the mirror and left the palace to do the king's bidding. But on the way to the E-sikil, the goddess Inanna appeared to him and blocked his way. "You must not go into the E-sikil! The E-sikil is the House of Purity, and you are stained by blood! Do not enter that House!"

And so it was that when Sargon arrived at the E-sikil, he would not enter but rather waited at the gate for the smith to come to him. Sargon delivered the mirror and returned to the palace unharmed. He resumed his duties as cupbearer, and the king said nothing to him of what the errand to the smith was intended to accomplish.

Five days passed, but not more than ten, and again, King Ur-Zababa had a frightening dream. He understood what it foretold, but he did not tell anyone else about it.

Now, in the days of Ur-Zababa, writing had been invented for some time. Scribes would write with a stylus on soft clay, and when the clay was dry, the tablet could be stored or delivered. It was common for people to exchange writings in this way, but as of yet, they did not put the tablets inside envelopes. One day, Ur-Zababa sent Sargon on a mission to deliver a tablet of writing to Lugalzagesi, the King of Uruk. The message on the tablet asked Lugalzagesi to kill Sargon.

[Here the story breaks off, and the few lines about Lugalzagesi that remain are fragmented. Presumably the rest of the story would have told us how Sargon evaded being murdered a second time and how he came to take Ur-Zababa's throne and thus begin the foundation of his empire.]

Here's another book that I think you'd be interested in:

And another one...

Bibliography

Barton, George A. *Miscellaneous Babylonian Inscriptions.* New Haven: Yale University Press, 1918.

Black, Jeremy et al. *The Literature of Ancient Sumer.* Oxford: Oxford University Press, 2004.

———— *The Electronic Text Corpus of Sumerian Literature* (http://www-etcsl.orient.ox.ac.uk/), Oxford 1998- .

Cohen, Sol. *Enmerkar and the Lord of Aratta.* PhD Dissertation. University of Pennsylvania. 1973.

Cooper, Jerrold S., and Wolfgang Heimpel. "The Sumerian Sargon Legend." *Journal of the American Oriental Society* 103/1 (1983): 67-82.

Echlin, Kim. *Inanna: A New English Version.* Toronto: Penguin Books, 2015.

Gadotti, Alhena. *Gilgamesh, Enkidu, and the Netherworld and the Sumerian Gilgamesh Cycle.* Boston: De Gruyter, Inc., 2014.

George, Andrew, trans. *The Epic of Gilgamesh: The Babylonian Epic Poem and Other Texts in Akkadian and Sumerian.* London: Penguin Books, Ltd., 2000.

Hallo, William W., ed. *The Context of Scripture: Canonical Compositions, Monumental Inscriptions, and Archival Documents from the Biblical World.* 3 Vols. Boston: Brill, 2003.

Hooke, Samuel Henry. *Middle Eastern Mythology.* Baltimore: Penguin Books, 1963.

Kramer, Samuel Noah. "The Sumerian Deluge Myth: Reviewed and Revised." *Anatolian Studies* 33 (1983): 115-121.

———. "Interim Report on Work at the Museum at Istanbul." *Bulletin of the American Schools of Oriental Research* 104 (1946): 8-12.

———. *Sumerian Mythology: A Study of Spiritual and Literary Achievement in the Third Millennium B. C.* Philadelphia: The American Philosophical Society, 1944.

———. *Gilgamesh and the* Huluppu-*Tree: A Reconstructed Sumerian Text.* Chicago: University of Chicago Press, 1938.

Lambert, W. G. *Babylonian Creation Myths.* Winona Lake: Eisenbrauns, 2013.

Langdon, Stephen Herbert. *Mythology of All Races.* Vol. 5: *Semitic.* New York: Cooper Square Publishers, 1964.

———. *Sumerian Epic of Paradise, the Flood, and the Fall of Man.* Philadelphia: University of Pennsylvania University Museum, 1915.

Leeming, David Adams. *The World of Myth: An Anthology.* Oxford: Oxford University Press, 1990.

Leick, Gwendolyn. *Sex and Eroticism in Mesopotamian Literature.* London: Routledge, 1994.

———. *A Dictionary of Ancient Near Eastern Mythology.* London: Routledge, 1991.

Mark, Joshua J. "Sargon of Akkad." *Ancient History Encyclopedia*, 2 September 2009. https://www.ancient.eu/Sargon_of_Akkad/.

Meador, Betty De Shong. *Inanna, Lady of Largest Heart: Poems of the Sumerian High Priestess Enheduanna.* Austin: University of Texas Press, 2000.

Pritchard, James B., ed. *Ancient Near Eastern Texts Relating to the Old Testament.* 3rd ed. Princeton: Princeton University Press, 1969.

Wolkstein, Diane, and Samuel Noah Kramer. *Inanna, Queen of Heaven and Earth: Her Stories and Hymns from Sumer.* New York: Harper & Row, 1983.

Dalley, Stephanie, trans. *Myths from Mesopotamia: Creation, The Flood, Gilgamesh, and Others.* Rev. ed. Oxford: Oxford University Press, 2000.

Ehrlich, Carl S., ed. *From an Antique Land: An Introduction to Ancient Near Eastern Literature.* Lanham: Rowman & Littlefield Publishers, Inc., 2009.

Ferry, David. *Gilgamesh: A New Rendering in English Verse.* New York: The Noonday Press, 1993.

Fessenden, Marissa. "Iraqi Museum Discovers Missing Lines from the Epic of Gilgamesh." **Smithsonian.com**, 7 October 2015.

Foster, Benjamin R. *Before the Muses: An Anthology of Akkadian Literature.* 3rd ed. Bethesda: CDL Press, 2005.

George, Andrew R. *The Babylonian Gilgamesh Epic.* Volume I: *Introduction, Critical Edition, and Cuneiform Texts.* Oxford: Oxford University Press, 2003.

Hallo, William W., ed. *The Context of Scripture: Canonical Compositions, Monumental Inscriptions, and Archival Documents from the Biblical World.* 3 Vols. Boston: Brill, 2003.

Heidl, Alexander. *The Babylonian Genesis: The Story of Creation.* 2nd ed. Chicago: University of Chicago Press, 1963.

King, L. W. *The Seven Tablets of Creation: or, The Babylonian and Assyrian Legends Concerning the Creation of the World and of Mankind.* Vol. 1. London: Luzac and Co., 1902.

Lambert, W. G. *Babylonian Creation Myths.* Winona Lake: Eisenbrauns, 2013.

Langdon, Stephen Herbert. *Mythology of All Races.* Vol. 5: *Semitic.* New York: Cooper Square Publishers, 1964.

Leeming, David. *The Oxford Companion to World Mythology.* Oxford: Oxford University Press, 2005.

———. *The World of Myth: An Anthology.* Oxford: Oxford University Press, 1990.

Leick, Gwendolyn. *A Dictionary of Ancient Near Eastern Mythology.* London: Routledge, 1991.

Mason, Herbert. *Gilgamesh: A Verse Narrative.* New York: Mentor Books, 1972.

Mitchell, Stephen. *Gilgamesh: A New English Version.* New York: Free Press, 2004.

Pritchard, James B., ed. *Ancient Near Eastern Texts Relating to the Old Testament.* 3rd ed. Princeton: Princeton University Press, 1969.

Rogers, Robert William, trans. and ed. *Cuneiform Parallels to the Old Testament.* New York: Eaton & Mains, 1912.

Spence, Lewis. *Myths & Legends of Babylon and Assyria.* London: G. G. Harrap, 1916.

Glossary

Abu	God created by **Ninhursag**
Adgarkidu	Daughter of the god **Numushda** and the goddess **Namrat**; wife of the god **Martu**
Aga	King of the city-state of **Kish**; ruled c. 2600 BCE
Amorites	Ancient nomadic people from what is now Syria
An	God of the sky; supreme Sumerian deity; son of **Apsu** and **Namma**; one of the **Annunaki**
Annunaki	The greater or elder gods
Anzu Bird	Mythical lion-headed bird creature
Apsu, the	Dwelling-place of **Enki**; also refers to both groundwater and the freshwater marshes of Sumer
Aratta	Mythical city that was very wealthy; rival to **Uruk** and **Kulaba**
Aruru	Another name for **Ninhursag**
Asag, the	Monstrous demon-creature defeated by **Ninurta**
Azimua	Goddess created by **Ninhursag**; wife of

	Ningishzida
Babylon	Ancient Mesopotamian city in what is now Iraq
Bau	Goddess of healing and consort of **Ninurta**
Belishtikal	Bronze-smith in the story of **Sargon** and **Ur-Zababa**
Bihartura	Soldier in the army of **Gilgamesh**
Dilmun	In Sumerian myth, a type of earthly paradise; in actuality was a region and culture on the eastern edge of the Arabian Peninsula along the Persian Gulf
Dumuzi	Shepherd-god who becomes the husband of **Inanna**
E-kur	Mythical house of the god **Enlil** in **Nippur**; also refers to the physical temple built by the Sumerians for the worship of Enlil
E-sikil	Temple mentioned in the story of **Sargon** and **Ur-Zababa**
Ebih	Mountain in the Zagros Range; in myth it refuses to bend the knee to **Inanna** and is punished for it
Elam	Ancient country on the northeastern shore of the Persian Gulf in what is now

	Iran
Enbilulu	God of canals; son of **Enlil** and **Ninlil**
Enegir	City mentioned in the myth of the journey of **Nanna** to **Nippur**
Enheduanna	Daughter of **Sargon of Akkad**, high priestess of **Inanna** and **Nanna** in **Ur**, first named author in history
Enki	"Lord Earth"; creator god and trickster, primarily associated with water; lives in the **Apsu**; son of **An** and **Namma**; one of the **Annunaki**
Enkidu	Companion and servant of **Gilgamesh**
Enkimdu	One of several Sumerian agricultural gods
Enlil	"Lord Air"; chief god of the Sumerian pantheon; lives in the **E-kur**; one of the **Annunaki**
Enmebaragesi (i)	Sister of **Gilgamesh**
Enmebaragesi (ii)	Historical king of the city-state of **Kish** and father of **Aga**
Enmerkar	Pseudo-historical king of **Uruk**; supposed father of **Lugalbanda**; supposed grandfather of **Gilgamesh**
Enshagag	God created by **Ninhursag**; given **Dilmun** as his domain

Ensuhkeshdanna	Mythical king of the city-state of **Aratta**; rival to **Enmerkar**
Ereshkigal	Goddess of the Underworld
Gilgamesh	Mythical hero; likely based on a historical Sumerian king who became deified and mythologized; supposed son of **Lugalbanda** and grandson of **Enmerkar**
Hamazu	Place mentioned as home of the sorcerer **Urgirinuna** in the story of **Enmerkar** and **Ensuhkeshdanna**
Huluppu Tree	Mythical tree rescued from a river by **Inanna**; possibly a willow tree
Huwawa	Mythical being sent to guard the **Mountain of Cedar** by **Enlil**; captured by **Gilgamesh** and slain by **Enkidu**
Id-kura	The river that separates the land of the living from the Underworld
Igigi	The lesser or younger gods
Inab	City mentioned in the story of the marriage of **Martu**
Inanna	Goddess of fertility, procreation, and war; often identified with the planet Venus; one of the **Annunaki**
Isimud	Adviser to **Enki**

Kalkal	Gatekeeper of the **E-kur** in **Nippur**
Ki-ur	Place mentioned in the myth of **Enlil** and **Ninlil**
Kish	Ancient Mesopotamian city between the Tigris and Euphrates Rivers in what is now Iraq
Kulaba	Another name for **Uruk**
Larsa	City mentioned in the story of the journey of **Nanna** to **Nippur**
Lilith	A demon-woman who inhabits the **huluppu tree**
Lugalbanda	Pseudo-historical king of **Uruk** and mythical hero; supposed father of **Gilgamesh** and son of **Enmerkar**
Lugalzagesi	Last king of Sumer before the conquest of **Sargon of Akkad**
Lulubi Mountains	Part of the Zagros range, now on the border between Iraq and Iran
Magan	Place mentioned in the story of **Enki** and **Ninhursag**; may have referred to Upper Egypt
Martu	God who represents the **Amorite** people
mikku	Stick used in an ancient Sumerian ball game

Mountains of Cedar	Mythical place where the creature **Huwawa** lives
Namma	Mother goddess; wife and mother of **An**; mother of **Enki**
Namrat	Wife of the god **Numushda**
Namtar	God of fate; vizier to **Ereshkigal**
Nanna	God of the moon; son of **Enlil** and **Ninlil**; one of the **Annunaki**
Nazi	Goddess of justice and commerce; daughter of **Ninhursag** and **Enki**
Nergal	God of war; consort of **Ereshkigal**; son of **Enlil** and **Ninlil**
Ninazu	"Lord Healer"; son of **Enlil** and **Ninlil**; god of boundaries
Ningirida	Goddess of **Enegir**
Ningishzida	"Lord of the Good Tree"; god associated with the Underworld
Ninhursag	"Lady of the Wild Hills"; creator goddess and consort of **Enki**; one of the **Annunaki**
Ninkasi	Goddess who fulfills wishes
Ninkura	"Lady of the Land"; daughter of **Enki** and **Ninsar**
Ninlil	"Lady Air"; consort of **Enlil**; mother of

	Nanna, Nergal, Enbilulu, and Ninazu
Ninmah	Another name for Ninhursag
Ninsar	Daughter of Enki and Ninhursag
Ninsikila	"Lady of Purity"; daughter of Enki; associated with Dilmun in the story of Enki and Ninhursag
Ninsun	"Lady of the Wild Cows"; mother of Gilgamesh and wife of Lugalbanda
Ninsutu	Goddess created by Ninhursag; consort of Ninazu
Ninti	Goddess created by Ninhursag; associated with calendars
Nintul	God created by Ninhursag; lord of Magan
Ninunuga	Goddess of Shuruppag
Ninurta	Hero-god of agriculture; associated with legal judgement; son of Enlil and Ninhursag; slayer of the Asag and bearer of the Sharur
Nippur	City in ancient Sumer between the Tigris and Euphrates Rivers in what is now Iraq
Nisaba	Goddess associated with grain; also seen as a patroness of scribes
Numushda	God mentioned in the story of the

	marriage of **Martu**; father of **Adgarkidu** and consort of **Namrat**
Nunbarshegunu	Mother of **Ninlil**
Nuska	Adviser to **Enlil**; titled "Master Builder of the E-kur" in the story of Enlil and **Ninlil**
Peshtur	Sister of **Gilgamesh**
pukku	Ball used for an ancient Sumerian game
Rimush	Brother of **Enheduanna**
Sagburu	A "wise woman" of **Uruk** who defeats the sorcerer **Urgirinuna**
Sargon of Akkad	Historical king and creator of the Akkadian Empire
Seven, the	Divine warriors each having different attributes
Sharur, the	The sentient battle mace belonging to **Ninurta**
Sherida	Goddess mentioned in the story of the journey of **Nanna** to **Nippur**; consort of **Utu**
Shuruppag	City in ancient Sumer mentioned in the story of the journey of **Nanna** to **Nippur**
Sin	Another name for **Nanna**

Subir	Region in Upper Mesopotamia
Suen	Another name for **Nanna**
Tummal	City in ancient Sumer mentioned in the story of the journey of **Nanna** to **Nippur**
Umul	Creature created by **Enki** in his contest with **Ninmah**; either a severely disabled adult or the first baby
Ur	Ancient Sumerian city on the south bank of the Euphrates in what is now Iraq
Ur-Zababa	King of **Kish**
Urgirinuna	Sorcerer who tries to help **Ensuhkeshdanna** win his contest with **Enmerkar**
Uruk	Ancient Sumerian city; home to **Enmerkar**, **Lugalbanda**, and **Gilgamesh**; rival to **Aratta**
Uttu	Goddess of weaving; daughter of **Enki** and **Ninkura**
Utu	God of the sun
Zabu Mountains	Ancient name for the Zagros Mountains, which run across the southern part of Turkey and then turn southeast to run between Iran and Iraq and from there along the eastern shore

	of the Persian Gulf
Zangara	God of dreams

Translations of names taken from Gwendolyn Leick, A Dictionary of Ancient Near Eastern Mythology *(London: Routledge, 1991).*

www.ingramcontent.com/pod-product-compliance
Lightning Source LLC
Chambersburg PA
CBHW070046230426
43661CB00005B/787